SPOT GARDENS

SPOT GARDENS

A Guide for Creating and Planting Miniature Gardens, Indoors and Outdoors

by

Dr. Robert E. Atkinson

DAVID McKAY COMPANY, INC.   *New York*

SPOT GARDENS

CONTENTS

INTRODUCTION:
What Are Spot Gardens?   vii

I. ENTRANCES   3
*How to Make Your Front Door More Inviting
Indoors and Out*

II. WALLS AND FENCES   25
*Drape and Embellish Them with Plants
and Flowers*

III. SHADE   51
Gardening Under Trees

IV. WATER   65
How Water Can Add Excitement

V. PATHS AND FLOORS   83
Walk on Beauty

VI. PRIVATE PATIOS   103
Outdoor Living Areas and Atriums

VII. THE SHORES   123
Plants and Flowers Beside Oceans and Lakes

VIII. ROCK GARDENS   139
       Planting with Pebbles, Boulders, and Stones

  IX. MOUNDS   159
       Make Your Level Garden More Interesting

   X. PORTABLE GARDENS   165
       Transform a Drab or Barren Spot
       Indoors and Out

  XI. TROPICAL PLANTINGS   195
       Hardy Plants with the Bold Look of
       the Tropics

 XII. ORIENTAL INFLUENCE   217
       Easy Maintenance with Japanese Gardens

XIII. KITCHEN GARDENS   239
       Useful and Edible Plants Close at Hand

 XIV. ART   251
       The Crowning Touch

       INDEX   269

CONTENTS

INTRODUCTION

What Are Spot Gardens?

"Spot gardening" is a new term coined to describe a small area, which by intensive planting at very little cost or effort can be turned into an exciting and colorful accent. It refers to just one particular small area of the house or garden where you can lavish care and, without too great a demand on your time, bring all the joys of gardening on a more extravagant scale. The term "pocket garden" was considered and discarded because of the similarity to the "pocket parks" now becoming popular. This book will furnish ideas, and, through pictures, show exactly how to reproduce garden spots that have a gemlike quality. Any person, no matter how busy, can concentrate on one small spot and, through a careful choice of plants suitable to the area, turn it into a microcosm of nature.

Many plants for your spot gardens originally came from the remote regions of the earth, and there are many recent imports entirely new to this country. We can vicariously travel all over the world in selecting our plantings. We can travel back in time by recalling the plants and flowers that stir forgotten memories of childhood. This nostalgia is a wonderful experience savored only by a thoughtful person who has the interest to create his own spot garden.

There are many practical rewards for making spot gardens but the esthetic benefits are by far the most important. In this day and age, expressions of our own individuality are among the most gratifying ways to satisfy a basic human need. The spot garden, whether a shrine or other artistic creation, enables us to articulate our feelings.

The wonder of nature, or awe at its intensity, the tremendous variety of textures, shapes, forms, and the thrill of the myriad of colors and tones—all these reflect the diversity of mankind and enable us to relate to others. A garden can emphasize the creative urge that gives us greater insight into ourselves and greater appreciation for our environment.

All locations in the garden and house that need to be cleverly or originally dealt with are the province of this book. Just satisfactory plantings are not enough. The high cost of land and rising taxes make every bit of space extremely valuable and you should be getting the utmost return from each precious segment of your home and garden.

All of this refurbishing, unlike structural additions and improvements, can be done without an increase in assessed valuation and a commensurate increase in taxes. You can add thousands of dollars in value and features that often result in quick sales by sensitive planning. Plantings increase in beauty and worth each year, adding immeasurably to the enjoyment of your surroundings.

Sometimes we think that balconies, cement patios, and wooden platforms where soil is not available, cannot be planted, but the increased use of container plants has opened up ways to stylishly furnish any area that has light from the sky. Even indoors, dim hallways can be brightened with plants in planters, especially if you move them outdoors during the summer.

Vegetation will cover unsightly structures and bare spots with a verdant blanket if left alone, but if discrimination is used in the selection of plantings, the results can be surprising. A large expanse of bare walls, concrete monoliths and wooden fences can be softened and beautified with flowers and foliage.

Your spot garden can be a jewel that reflects the changing seasons and keeps you in tune with the universe.

SPOT
GARDENS

Chapter I

ENTRANCES

How to Make Your Front Door
More Inviting Indoors and Out

Instead of standardized planting that makes an entrance look like a business office, or worse, as impersonal as a jetport passenger lounge, your front entry can express your personality. And, in addition, it will give your home a distinctive appearance that sets it off from all the other houses in the neighborhood. Sometimes a group planting can work wonders. Frequently, plants in pots set here and there add a deft touch that will be effective, but it always requires thought and careful planning. Occasionally, minor refurbishing is needed.

Plantings are the key to making yours a "friendly" entrance;

A dark entrance such as this one offers an opportunity and a challenge for planting. It is a chance to make plants in bloom last longer and the use of plants in containers can dress the entrance at all seasons of the year. In spring, depicted here, various bulbs such as tulips, hyacinths, daffodils, can be used. Cyclamen, cineraria, calceolaria, and azaleas, which can be obtained from florists, will also brighten the entrance. Many annuals in full bloom such as petunias and marigolds are also favorites. Now chrysanthemums which last for months are available at almost all seasons but are usually less expensive in the fall, during their natural blooming time.

ENTRANCE

3

Ferns, aralia, and begonias are used here to provide accents in a shaded entry. Other good choices are pieris, daphne, rhododendron, mahonia, and osmanthus. In the sun, blue fescue and juniper thrive. These are both very hardy and can be grown in any area.

decorative screens, windows with a grill, interesting mosaic patterns in paving or other ornaments will help give the necessary impact. Plants that have a sculptured appearance, permeating fragrance, pleasing compatible colors, or beauty of form are the ones to choose. It is well to select those whose intricate features may be seen only at close range, for the visitor may spend many unoccupied moments approaching the entrance and waiting for the doorbell to be answered. Larger specimens should be chosen to dress the entrance as seen from the street, for it is usually the face that is seen by everyone who passes.

Entrances are often dark and shadowy and these bring special problems in plant selection. The roof overhang and narrow confines can make an entry almost as dark as the indoors, so plants need to be just as carefully chosen. The only way to have blooming plants continually, throughout the growing season, is to use container plants and move them to the entry when they are in blossom. This is most easily accomplished with annuals and bulbs but several low-growing shrubs can be used in this way too. Plants that come to you on special occasions such as birthdays and Mother's Day, or on Easter and other holidays, can keep an almost continuous supply of blooming plants if they are used at the entrance or inside the front door. Many homes have planters in the dark hallway that leads to the entry. This is often the worst place in the house to grow plants because of the lack of light, and unfortunately many have filled those planters with artificial plants.

This is an ideal place for blooming azaleas, lilies, chrysanthemums, and other florist gift plants. They will hold their flowers longer in this dark cool location and serve the double purpose of a cordial welcome and a fond goodbye to entering and departing friends.

For permanent exterior plantings, several shrubs enliven the scene during their blooming season. Choice fragrant shrubs include sweet pepperbush, azalea, andromeda, witch-hazel, some viburnums, daphne, rhododendron (*R. fragrantissima*), osmanthus (sweet-olive), night blooming jasmine, brunfelsia, banana shrub, sarcococca, and star jasmine. Other blooming shrubs are Hills-of-Snow and oak-leaved hydrangea, enkianthus, fothergilla, mountain-laurel, abelia, and camellia. Those with bright berries include cotoneaster, barberry, holly, ardisia, skimmia, mahonia (holly-grape), and many viburnums. Shrubs with striking foliage include holly, stephanandra, aucuba, and aralia.

Vines around and over the front door are a pleasing embellish-

(Left) A sunny entrance can be made enchanting with plantings of fragrant hybrid tea or floribunda roses. The bushes must be pruned drastically so that branches do not invade the path. Thorny plants have a tendency to reach out and grab unwary visitors and fierce rose thorns can make deep scratches. If the space is large enough, a hybrid tea that blooms consistently might be suitable but in a smaller space one of the floribundas would be the choice.

(Below) A Japanese feeling of serenity is conferred by the austere black-and-white contrasts of this entrance. White gravel beds line the exposed aggregate walks. White dusty miller (far side of walk) and (near side) gray billbergia are chosen for their contrasting textures. The drooping billbergia is an indoor/outdoor plant in cold winter areas. On the wall a simple espalier takes full advantage of the narrow bed offered between the garage and sidewalk.

The handsome translucent gate dresses an otherwise unexciting entrance. Pines, especially when the "candles" are long, are good sturdy plants near an entrance. Here the ground is covered with smooth river pebbles to serve as a mulch. In the background a spruce is pruned in bonsai style though not miniature. This is an effective treatment for overgrown multiple-trunked tall shrubs that gives them more character.

10

Succulents used here for easy maintenance can be duplicated in a colder climate using hardier species of Yucca and Sempervivum. Unfortunately, the dominant element on the right, Agave attenuata *has no hardier counterpart. However, daylilies or cannas with their exciting colors could make an equally appealing scene. This species of* Agave *does well in a container and might be stored in a heated garage for the winter season, and wheeled out to the entrance in early spring. It will survive temperatures down to twenty degrees above zero.*

Flowering shrubs like the one shown here, romantically named yesterday-today-and-tomorrow, give an eye-catching beauty to the entrance. If it is also fragrant, as this one is (also called Brunfelsia), it has an added appeal. Some that belong in this category are sweet-olive, mock-orange, the honey-suckle, azalea, daphne, some viburnums, lavender, rhododendron, sarco-cocca, and lilac. The tree shown here is the Hollywood twisted juniper.

ment that give the entrance a soft and appealing appearance. If flowering vines are chosen, the effect may be almost devastating during the blooming season. The danger here is overdoing or concealing good architectural features instead of enhancing them. A few choice vines may be mentioned as possibilities; the array headed by wisteria, and including clematis, honeysuckle, climbing hydrangea, star jasmine, Carolina yellow jessamine, the true jasmines, and several species of *Bignonia*. Morning-glory, sweet-peas, cup-and-saucer, and other annuals can be used for temporary effects. Non-blooming vines are ivy, Boston-ivy, Virginia creeper, grape-ivy, and evergreen grape.

For groundcovers which are suitable for dark entries, and at the same time have colorful blooms, consider violets, rock-cress, ajuga (bugleweed), hosta (plantain-lily), Carpathian and Serbian bluebell, leadwort, golden star, creeping myrtle (periwinkle), lily-of-the-valley, bunchberry, oconee-bells, strawberry-geranium and other saxifragas, primroses, trailing arbutus, and mazus. Those with interesting foliage are ivy, wild ginger, pachysandra (Japanese spurge), galax, leopard plant, barrenwort, Corsican hellebore, alum root (coral-bells), dead nettle, lily-turf (especially the variegated forms), lungwort, foamflower, mondo-grass, and Sprenger's asparagus. Many kinds of low-growing ferns also fit in this category.

ENTRY WALKS

The walk is the first important feature of entrances. A straight concrete sidewalk like all the others on the street is not only dull but uninviting. It may not be wide enough for two people to walk side by side. To make it more impressive and more functional it is necessary to widen it. If the widening is done with brick or some texture that contrasts with the concrete, the new walk will also be distinctive. A gentle curve makes a walk seem more interesting and less rigid.

Flower borders will soften the severity of the concrete walk and make the entrance more exciting. A curving line of trees or shrubs will help direct the eye to the front door.

Because most visitors arrive by car, your driveway may be as important as your walk. Sometimes when the garage is incorporated into the house the driveway and the front walk are joined. This wide expanse of concrete or macadam needs special treatment to keep it from becoming an overwhelming element. Breaking up the paved

(Right) A little bed around a lamppost or mailbox gives an opportunity for original plantings. Here variegated ivy is used as a groundcover underneath large mounds of Chinese holly. Bittersweet could be substituted for the holly or one of the new dwarf firethorns (pyracantha) such as 'Tom Thumb.' Ajuga or prostrate rosemary would also be suitable. The shrublike lavender-cotton or santolina, which comes in white or green, is very ornamental.

(Below) Garage doors may be decorated with initials or designs to give a unique character to a home. Here a Chinese scroll and a ladder design on each side fight the monotony of a wide expanse of white. The trellislike lines on either side make the wide door appear more narrow and give the central design more meaning.

14

16

(Left) An indoor-outdoor plant in a ceramic planter is adapted to both locations. Aralia's handsome leaves are an interior decoration without equal. The plant grows easily in any shaded location outdoors and can be maintained in a dark spot indoors. The ceramic planter will break in freezing temperatures, so in such climates it is best to take it indoors.

(Below) A light fence screen made of plastic panels and dark wood gives the feeling of Japanese shoji. Plastic sheets serve as a more practical material for this door that would have been heavy and unwieldy if it were made of solid wood. The design is more becoming to the style of architecture and creates an oriental mood.

17

18

The use of wide expanses of patterned glass in contemporary homes, especially at the entrance, makes an ideal spot for the growth of tall indoor plants. These may attain full ceiling height for a more dramatic effect. Here a fiddle-leafed fig, underplanted with begonias and clivia is in a floor-level planter. The lack of an above-ground container keeps the huge plant in scale. A flagstone floor prevents damage from accidentally spilled water.

surface into modular segments with four-by-four headers is one solution, or just varying the design and texture of the paving is another. But the best method is to provide large or small out-of-the-way areas for planting.

For those who will park in the street, it is wise to have a gravel strip or squares of stepping stones where they will alight. This not only saves your lawn in the parkway strip but also prevents your visitors from getting shoes, dresses, and trousers soiled by the mud or dust.

Most guests arrive when it is dark, so it is important how your entry is illuminated. A simple porch or door light is enough but when steps or uneven paving blocks are used, path lights are desirable. Sometimes the best effects are created when the entire front landscape is lit. Walls of translucent plastic and handsome fixtures add grace and beauty to the entrance at night. An entry planter with lights strategically placed to shine against the wall, casting giant shadows of plants in the foreground is a device that should be used more often. It dramatizes the entrance more effectively than any other means. For evening parties, a border of lights from the street to the front door can be made by setting candles in a layer of sand in the bottom of brown paper bags.

In modern homes with an attached garage the double doors often are a dull and unattractive expanse about which little can be done with planting. It offers, however, a great opportunity for original decoration.

The best ideas are derived from some design element used in the architecture of the house or in its interior decoration. It is easy to come up with bamboo designs for houses that display the Chinese or Japanese influence, and plywood can run the gamut in the modern homes. Ranch-style and rustic homes require the use of driftwood and boards with bark attached, in keeping with their style. Patterns made with nails or studs add interest in most any setting.

House numbers in giant size, mosaics of tile, pebbles, or shells are effective if tastefully done. Strips of wood in a decorative pattern set inside an open frame backed by plywood can add the needed strength to a broad garage door.

A night garden conveys a special feeling of privacy. Some are enclosed with screening, if insects are a problem.

Palms are excellent subjects for indoor use but most need abundant light to stay healthy. Those such as the Chamaedorea elegans *'Bella' or* Neanthe bella *shown here are good choices, as are the lady palm and the standard palms (the so-called* Kentia palm) *used in hotel lobbies. The tall slender lady palms adapted to dark locations are best used for vertical accents. Its bamboo-like canes and clumping habit make it an outstanding accent.*

(Hedrich-Blessing)

Chapter II

WALLS AND FENCES

Drape and Embellish Them with Plants and Flowers

The great advantage of planting on a wall is the softening of harsh architectural features. A dull or barren surface can be brought alive with a single vine, or group of appropriate plants. These pockets or half baskets on a wall can have the same effect outdoors as pictures and other wall decorations have indoors. Vines may hang like draperies or veil like curtains.

When we say "wall" we may be speaking of any one of the many types that appear in the average garden. There are of course many kinds of fences, but every garden has structures. The walls of a house or garage may face in any direction of the compass. Each exposure poses problems of plant selection and each kind of material of which the wall is composed—brick or stone, wood or stucco—has its own problems or failings.

The fences around a bedroom or bathroom garden are of critical importance in design (see chapter VI).

Vines that drape over walls include bittersweet, blue leadwort, ground morning-glory, and periwinkle. Here Confederate jasmine cascades over a brick wall. In the background an informal espalier covers a wall in an interesting and unusual pattern.

A wall on Henry Ford's home in Dearborn, Michigan, is softened by a climbing hydrangea. Although the whole wall is covered with ivy, the hydrangea itself originates from a single location bordering the flagstone terrace at the chimney corner. Boston-ivy is the most common leafy concealment.

Rather than concealing, a clematis is displayed to greatest effect on a stone wall bordering a cement terrace. Only a narrow space is provided for the vine roots to find needed sustenance, but the aboveground parts extend widely in each direction. The flowering aspect of this vine is its most lovely feature. Other tracery vines that flower are Carolina yellow jessamine, coral vine, cypress vine, canary-bird-vine, and silver lace.

27

(Right) A bower of bamboo provides sufficient support for light vines such as the English ivy used here. They can quickly create a vertical screen wherever needed. Other dainty vines for trellises are Allegheny vine, Madeira, cup-and-saucer, clematis, cypress vine, and clockvine.

(Below) Yellow trumpet vine gracefully covers a brick wall, making a forbidding structure soft and colorful. Other vines which fasten to brick walls include ivy, creeping fig, and flame vine. A hardy type is the trumpet-creeper which uses aerial roots to fasten to masonry walls. Freezing weather kills it to the ground but it grows quickly from the undamaged crown. Other very hardy vines are wintercreeper and Chinese trumpet.

STRUCTURE WALLS

All bare walls offer an opportunity to the gardener that should be utilized to the fullest. Brick walls, because they don't have to be painted, may be covered with vines that attach directly to them. Some of these are Virginia creeper, wintercreeper, English ivy, Boston ivy, trumpetcreeper, climbing hydrangea, cat's-claw, flame vine, and creeping fig.

But don't plant any of them against a wooden wall unless you never intend to paint it. The removal of the vine is enough of a chore but to clean up the attached tendrils is practically impossible. It is best to use a trellis or wire frame and choose among the many twining vines or the tendril climbers that do not hold tightly to the surface. The close proximity of vine and siding promotes dry rot and favors termites, because of the moisture held by the vegetation. Stucco also offers problems; although it doesn't have to be painted as often as wood, it does need it occasionally.

Of all the exposures, the most difficult to get satisfactory growth is on a north wall, especially if a nearby house or overhanging tree reduces the sky light available. Of those that adhere to stone and brick, the most shade tolerant are ivy, wintercreeper, and Virginia creeper. Of the vines that do not cling, Dutchman's-pipe, grape, akebia, honeysuckle, and star jasmine are best.

For the south and west walls which are fully exposed to the hot summer sun, trumpetcreeper, morning-glory, roses, and wisteria are the best of the non-clinging types. Choice in a semitropical zone would be the flame vine and creeping fig, which adhere, and bougainvillea which does not. Do not allow the vine to reach the eaves, for some, especially wisteria, will get under the shingles and raise the roof!

RETAINING WALLS

These may be made of cinder block, concrete, or brick. You can choose vines which cover or plants that grow in the soil above and merely drape over the wall, softening the rigid structural lines. On a large retaining wall you may wish to use both vines that climb and those that hang, but for low walls certain pliable shrubs are the best choice for draping casually like a shawl. Rock cotoneaster, prostrate rose-

SPOT GARDENS

English ivy growing from a birdcage planter is a simple decoration that
makes this wall uniquely attractive. A variety of ivy with an unusual leaf
shape makes the decoration more interesting.

For an arbor nothing excels wisteria. When in bloom, the long drooping tassels produce a heavenly effect. Here a white variety is used to create an area for dining alfresco near Venice, Italy.

mary, barberry, primrose jasmine, lantana, and Cape plumbago are good. Juniper, English yew, weeping forsythia, and caragana are examples of other hardy kinds.

DRY WALLS

The most popular way to hold a steep bank is to construct a dry wall of rock, cinder blocks, or broken pieces of concrete, with soil between and no mortar. This wall is popular because you need no permit in most areas to build it. Cinder blocks with the open ends out is an ideal material.

For a wall higher than three feet, you need a footing of poured concrete eighteen to twenty-four inches wide and twelve inches deep. The surface need not be troweled, as it will be covered with soil. While the concrete cures, you can mix the soil to be used between the stones. A good mix is twenty-five percent sand, and ten percent humus, and the balance good garden soil that does not contain much clay.

Flat stones are best but broken concrete, rocks, bricks—laid in a lattice-work—and cinder blocks are also used. If you use flat flag-stones, the largest should be at the base. Tilt all rocks toward the hill and slant the wall backward, at the ratio of one inch to a foot of height. Have at least an inch of soil between rocks and set your plants in as the wall is built. Choose plants that are low and not too vigorous spreaders. Sempervivums and some sedums are ideal, as well as ajuga, Serbian bluebells, rock-cress, and several of the herbs. If you wish to add plants after the wall is finished, insert a crowbar between the rocks and poke the roots into the hole.

FENCES

Garden walls of wood or masonry may be treated as the walls of structures but split rail, chain link, lattices, and picket fences offer separate problems in the use of plants. Roses are best for rail fences, offering no interference with ventilation, no shading or reflection problems, to insure the healthiest, most vigorous plants. The climbing type of hybrid teas or floribundas flower most profusely when the cane is arched with the tip held below the main part of the stem. This

Prostrate rosemary exudes its remarkable fragrance toward all who approach this dwelling near Phoenix, Arizona. The dusty blue flowers add a delicate grace note. Other sprawling shrubs that might be chosen in this location, include lantana, cotoneaster, bearberry, junipers, barrenwort, and Natal-plum.

The easiest retaining wall to build is one made of rock or cement blocks loosely piled up and inclined slightly toward the top. Soil used in-between the rocks allows water to penetrate freely so no pressure builds up behind the wall. Here a flowering display is created by plants growing between the stones.

Succulents such as hardy sedum (Sedum rupestre), echeveria and semper-vivum are excellent as used here between flat flagstones to hold a steep slope that would otherwise wash in heavy rains.

A traditional wood rail fence covered with fragrant hybrid tea roses makes a lovely picture from inside the house and maintains a trim beauty from the street. Gazanias used as a groundcover can be replaced with coreopsis or sun-rose in colder areas.

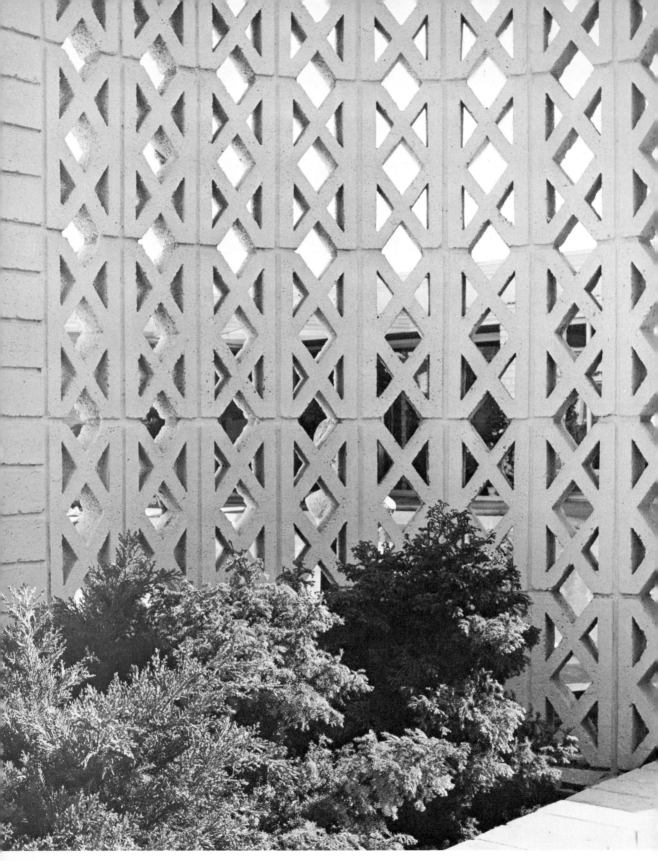

The classic appearance of the cement block screen has the blocks on end instead of the traditional and unimaginative horizontal fashion. It is enhanced by plantings of juniper, which are easily maintained yet good looking.

stimulates the development of side shoots (laterals) on which the flowers are borne. Certain climbing roses, such as the ramblers, are prodigious growers that can reach twenty feet in a single season. Their small flowers are borne in clusters, usually in midsummer, on the older shoots produced the previous year. Winter pruning removes these flower buds. 'Dorothy Perkins' and 'Crimson Rambler' are hardy in any climate. Less rampant "everblooming" types that flower on the current season's wood are 'New Dawn' and 'Blaze.' Carolina yellow jessamine and several twining jasmines are also excellent and have fragrance that rivals the finest roses. If you don't relish the idea of pruning thorny rose branches, choose among these substitutes.

Chain link fences may be covered completely by fast-growing annual vines or other non-woody species but it is best to avoid the rampant woody ones such as ivy because they are so difficult to remove. In subtropical areas, passion-vine is a favorite for this purpose, and the five-leaved akebia does equally well. Honeysuckle and silver lace vine also tend to cover completely and rapidly. The latter has become a great favorite even in polluted cities.

Sometimes, however, it is best to choose a vine that merely veils or only partly covers the wall in a decorative pattern. These soften rather than hide the fence. Clematis would be the best example. Cinnamon-vine is good in sun or shade but Kenilworth-ivy and Japanese hop thrive only in shade.

Best for lattices and trellises are ampelopsis, cobaea, clematis, clockvine, and climbing roses.

Arbors need large foliaged or enveloping vines which are strong growing. They require lots of room and strong supports as the weight develops, especially when the cover of snow is deep. Wisteria of course, comes first to mind, with Virginia creeper a close second. Dutchman's-pipe, and kudzu are other fast vigorous vines that will densely cover an arbor.

SCREENS

A growing trend that helps us accomplish our need for privacy is a short, strategically placed length of fence called a screen. These may be made of translucent plastic or may have louvers to invite cool breezes.

(Left) The unusual appearance of this brick wall is developed by combining insets of patterned wood. The see-through quality of the screen removes the forbidding aspects of the high wall. African iris and white petunias emphasize the white wall and add grace and natural beauty to an otherwise cold design.

(Below) A Japanese surrealist could not paint a more unique scene than is created with this translucent plastic screen. The Japanese iris behind the screen seems to reflect those in front of it, as in a smoky mirror.

41

The stem structures of vines are important design elements and should not be neglected or covered with leaves and branches. Here a honeysuckle is formally trained on a wall while the top is allowed to grow rampant. Other heavy enveloping vines that might be used in this fashion are Dutchman's-pipe, grape, jasmine, wisteria, and Virginia creeper.

42

Another informal espalier is achieved using the species of Calliandra known as Trinidad flame. Any shrub with a sprawling-type growth is adaptable to this technique. Flowering quince, rock-rose, cotoneaster, Russian olive, holly, primrose jasmine, buckthorn, winged-bark euonymus, blackhaw viburnum, and crab apples would also be good choices.

44

Espaliers require much time for training but an informal design shown here is less demanding. Pyracantha at least offers a dramatic white bloom in the spring followed by red, orange or yellow berries in the fall. About all of the pruning required for this pattern is removal of all branches which jut out from the fence and a few crossing branches.

Screens are not exclusively barriers to shield your patio activities from the neighbor's view. They can also give shelter from prevailing or cold winds and protect from the late afternoon sun. But perhaps the best use of a screen is to extend or heighten a masonry or wooden fence. Some localities have laws limiting the height of a fence to four feet and developers often provide cement-block walls that high. This does not ensure privacy and, until vines and trees have time to grow, the wall can be heightened by a lattice or louvers on the top of the four-foot fence or on a free-standing frame. To accommodate vines or espaliers, horizontal strands of wire set on the top of the fence will suffice. Free-standing rectangular or crossed beams may be used to build a frame to support the lighter non-woody vines. Because of the natural supportive structure of espaliers, they may be grown on a light frame.

ESPALIERS

High walls that surround your property create confined sensation that can border on claustrophobia. The penned-in feeling can be relieved by vines or certain shrubs trained in either formal or natural patterns on the wall. This is the art of espalier, developed in Europe in the sixteenth century. The original purpose was to use the heat of a southerly wall to allow the growth of fruits in colder areas than they would normally tolerate. Citrus, figs, peaches, plums, and other fruits were produced far beyond their climatic limitations. Others used this method to get fruit earlier than their competitors who grew it in the open.

Foundation plantings originally were used to soften the harsh lines of modern architecture. Most of these overpower or hide the good features and become so massive they are competing architectural elements themselves. All of the best features of a plant are displayed in an espalier—its beauty of flower and fruit, shape and texture of leaves, line and form of the stem. Added to this is the great advantage of using only a small amount of space.

Chapter III

SHADE

Gardening Under Trees

Many large shade trees have voracious shallow roots that make trouble for any plants that grow in the vicinity. All tree roots devour water and minerals, which must be supplied in increasing amounts. Fully grown trees are extremely valuable and deserve any changes that can be made to accommodate them.

The heavy absorption of water and minerals by tree roots may be alleviated by more fertilizer and more watering. Deep watering is essential to promote the growth of tree roots below the grass root zone. Deep watering means that the hose or sprinklers should run overnight. Even in dry desert areas, deep watering once a month is sufficient. Shallow root growth that competes with grasses, groundcovers, and flowers is favored when deep watering is omitted.

Some trees, notably cottonwood, willow, maple, and eucalyptus will fill the surface soil with fine roots that prevent any but the most vigorous ornamentals from thriving. Removal of these roots does little good; they quickly return. Once they are removed, however, deep

For the wild garden in a woods, the best plants are those native to the area such as the collection shown here—bunchberry, ginger, trillium and maianthemum. Partridge-berry, twinflower and violets are also possible in such a dell.

Carefree groundcovers under trees must be able to thrive in reduced light and compete with voracious tree roots for water and minerals. Few plants are better adapted for this than ivy. You can grow it farther north, well beyond its natural limits if you keep it on the ground. Runners that climb will not survive in severe winters, while prostrate ivy endures. Shown here is the variegated Algerian ivy, less hardy than the many forms of English ivy.

"Mother of thousands," Saxifraga stolonifera, *is a good spreading plant under trees in areas south of Pennsylvania in the East and south of Kansas in the Midwest. The tiny white flowers are borne in feathery sprays but the white-veined leaves are its chief ornamental attraction. Hardier substitutes would include ajuga, mondo-grass, moneywort, and Kenilworth-ivy.*

Ferns, of course, are excellent in shady locations and cannot be surpassed for gardens under trees. However, to relieve the monotonous green, color should be supplied wherever possible. Here a wax begonia is used. Coreopsis, plantain-lily, epimedium, bergenia, and helleborus each lend their particular charm.

Pots of cineraria can be obtained from florists and garden centers in the spring. These will give months of continuous bloom if the pots are sunken in the soil under trees. The predominantly blue colors of cineraria are especially effective in the shade.

(Left) For the health of a tree when the grade is lowered it is sometimes necessary to build a retaining wall. This used brick wall is in keeping with the design of the house. Ajuga thrives in the raised bed, with the advantage of good drainage.

(Below) A shade tree offers the most natural place to build a bench. A circular bench allows you to sit under the shady side in summer and the sunny side in winter, without moving the bench.

metal barriers of aluminum or tin keep the shallow roots out. However, deeper roots will go under the barrier and eventually take over.

Often the best solution is to select plants that compete with tree roots when there is sufficient water and nutrients for both. Grasses that thrive in the shade include the shade bluegrass (also called "rough stalked" or *Poa trivialis*), and meadow fescue. The latter is very coarse in texture. In subtropical areas, zoysia and St. Augustinegrass, are well suited to shady situations.

A Japanese garden (see chapter XII) may also be effective under trees.

Because the areas under trees may look barren and unattractive, this is where a spot garden can do wonders.

Matching plants with the type of shade you have is a challenge. It is easy to recognize the deep shade conferred by a building where the north sky is shielded by the low branches. This is almost the darkest location found in a garden, yet there are groundcovers adapted to this darkness. Among them are wild ginger, arum-root, sweet woodruff, lily-of-the-valley, barrenwort, helleborus, galax, wintergreen, ivy, dead nettle, mayflower, bunchberry, pachysandra, partridge-berry, oconee-bells, trailing arbutus, trillium, trailing myrtle, and the barren-strawberry.

Under the high arching branches of trees, you will find the condition known as light shade. Columbine, rock-cress, Carpathian blue-bell, leadroot, golden star, bleeding-heart, foxglove, shooting star, leopard's-bane, meadowsweet, crested iris, lily-turf, phlox, meadow-rue, foamflower, globeflower, and violet, do well in this location.

Warm and cool shade are still other qualities that may be used to describe areas where shadows abound. Caladiums, coleus, lobelia, torenia, daylily, mazus, hosta, ajuga, and coral-bells all need warm shade. Primrose, bergenia, and numerous other familiar plants delight in cool shadows. The many species of fern are, of course, ideal in the cool moist forest floor.

It may seem that in modern gardens a bench under a tree is not as useful as the bench on the patio.

But the best place for a bench is where you find people congregating, and bringing up chairs to accommodate them has become a constant chore. You will be amazed how many people a bench can

This long slotted bench built on modern lines is set among the ferns and flowers so they can be contemplated close at hand for hours or—minutes—whenever you have the spare time. No spot garden can be more perfect than this, especially if it is your own.

This raised bed supports a birch tree and a collection of succulents and bulbs, all of which benefit from the sharp drainage it provides. The sturdy wooden bench offers a place to sit and watch the activities on the lawn.

A water nymph plays in the pool amid rocks and succulent plants. This charming setting lends enjoyment all of its own.

A cork oak affords a rugged background for one of the best of the shade-loving flowering plants, impatiens. Azaleas, camellias and fuchsias also thrive in mild winter areas. For the colder climates, osmanthus (sweet-olive), summersweet, leucothoë, stephanandra and snowberry are dependable.

seat and you'll be relieved of the responsibility of rounding up chairs and putting them away when the crowd has left.

Remember when you select the place for a permanent bench that it should face the action. People resist sitting where they are removed from the activity but prefer to be surrounded by it. Fortunately a backless bench faces two ways and can double as a quiet conversational retreat if it is placed strategically.

Benches serve other functions than merely a place to sit. They make excellent dividers and are often used to terminate a vista or they can form a barrier near a steep bank or at the end of a deck. A bench may be used for sunbathing or as an end table, or it may become a display shelf for flowering potted plants.

Chapter IV

WATER

How Water Can Add Excitement

The sound of water tinkling or splashing is as welcome as the song of birds in the garden. The contemporary garden has flowing water instead of the placid reflecting pools of the previous decade. Perhaps this is to counteract the noise that pervades even the most quiet of towns and suburbs. The whine of jet engines, the pound of heavy trucks, and the screech of buses, all add to the ever present din of children playing. Some are satisfied with the beauty of the sky as seen in the water's surface, some rejoice in the sparkle of a fountain's whirling pattern. Many enhance their pools with brightly colored *koi* or goldfish; others with sprightly water-lilies.

Whether the water bubbles, spouts, or drips, depends on the outlet. The design of your fountain may be as intricate as a work of art or as simple as a spray head. The pool, too, may be a hollow scooped out of the ground and lined with black plastic film. But the fiber-glass pools, which originated in England, are much better and can be installed as easily as a bathtub. They are designed to be deep

A well-designed reflection pool with a birdbath and Grecian head decorate a formal setting. The lavish plantings of hydrangeas and chrysanthemums seem overdone but serve to illustrate its beauty.

WATER

65

If you use your ingenuity, pools may be tiny and yet support water-lilies. The principle used here is that although the leaves need light, roots grow as well or better in the dark. Thus the planter overhanging the pool takes nothing away from the water plants.

A small pool and waterfall adjacent to the house makes this tiny back yard come alive. The closeness of the neighbor's dwelling is overcome by the interest added to nearby features. Vines and trellises offer a vertical accent and translucent screens assure privacy.

67

The versatility of redwood is illustrated by this deck overhanging a pool of water-lilies and other water plants. The deck is made more cheerful by planters of chrysanthemums and juniper. Garden furniture, fences, planters, and the egg-crate shelter are all of redwood.

enough to grow water-lilies, and some are even equipped with circulating pumps and fountains. Inexpensive pumps are available at your garden center.

Here we are mainly concerned with the choice of the surrounding plants and this is most critical when a sizeable body of water, such as a swimming pool, is involved. Keeping leaves and debris from a pool is one of the chores to be avoided at all costs. There is also the problem of how to prevent the saline, chlorinated, pool water from splashing onto adjacent lawns and plantings.

HOW TO PREVENT DAMAGE FROM
SPLASHED POOL WATER

To protect plants around the perimeter of the pool, there must be adequate drainage for the water splashed on the apron. This can be done with a border of gravel or colored stones. If it is sufficiently wide and deep, it will absorb all the excess water. However, if the bottom is lined with plastic and it slopes to a sewer or to natural drainage, it may be reduced in size and depth but still take care of any amount of overflow.

To keep children from picking up the stones and throwing them into the pool (or, worse yet, through the windows) and to make the border smooth and flush with the surface of the apron, the rock can be covered with a hardware cloth grating.

More sophisticated and less noticeable is a device that hides the drainage line by leaving a narrow (one-half-inch) opening between the cement of the apron and the header board, and bringing the lawn or flower bed over the drain. The narrow slit is sufficient to accommodate the flow of water and allows the apron to be flushed with the hose without flooding the garden.

PLANTINGS ADJACENT TO A SWIMMING POOL

Unless a pool is situated at least a hundred yards from trees that drop their leaves, leaf removal will be a constant problem. If possible, you must choose plants that do not drop their leaves. In the warmer areas where swimming pools are more common, palm trees, bananas, dracaenas, giant bird-of-paradise flowers, and tree ferns serve as vertical accents but these can be used in cold climates only if brought out in tubs. About the only other choice here are hardy yuccas and some columnar junipers, spruce, and arborvitae. Hardy to Washington D.C., are some evergreen trees, including southern magnolia, which causes less of a leaf problem than deciduous trees.

Evergreen shrubs are also a good choice, although the total leaf-age from deciduous shrubs can usually be handled easily. However, for the immediate vicinity of the swimming pool ivies, ferns, daylilies, and the low junipers are best.

PLANTINGS FOR LILY PONDS

While a reflecting pool should be stark without overhanging plantings of any kind, to look natural a pond must be surrounded by water-loving plants. Some will grow in the water, some on the edge of the pool. They should be kept in scale: some of the miniature forms are best for small ponds. Miniature cattail is hardy everywhere, as is the sedge called "umbrella-palm." Horsetail, also called scouring rush (*Equisetum*), with its jointed stems is a handsome decoration. Some of the taros called "elephant's-ear" will kill back to the soil line but survive in areas where the ground does not freeze. The tubers can be lifted and stored over winter in the colder climates. A choice container plant near a pool, to be removed to warm quarters in winter, is the Egyptian papyrus. The tall one is for large ponds or swimming pools, while a dwarf type only two feet tall lends itself to small pools. Most beautiful of all poolside flowers is the Japanese iris. The exotic lotus make an exquisite scene. They are tall (three feet) and seldom bloom the first year, but they are extremely hardy. They must have six inches of water over them, and the tuber is planted only one or two inches deep with the tip out of the soil.

In order to have a balanced condition to maintain fish in your pond, it is necessary to have oxygenating plants in the water. The best of these, *Anacharis*, myriophyllum, vallisneria, and *Cabomba*, need deep water. There is a miniature *Sagittaria* that is excellent for shallow pools (less than twelve inches deep). Floating plants for shallow pools include *Azolla* (a moss-like plant), duckweed, water-hyacinth, and water-lettuce.

SPOT GARDENS   For tiny pools, the pygmy water-lilies and water-poppies, parrot's-

70

Another redwood deck backed by reed fencing for privacy, and covered with a handsome curved roof gives both shelter and a placid view. Low upkeep of water plants, rocks, and pebbles are featured. The plant in the foreground is purple heart (Setcreasea purpurea), *a relative of the wandering Jew, which could be used in its place.*

(Right) The water spouts from three spigots on a standpipe and tumbles from two levels into a pool. This interesting design for a recirculating pump gets the most from the power expended.

(Below) A garden room with its brick floor is given a new dimension by a sunken pool and waterfall. The pool, not light enough for water plants, is surrounded by tropical foliage, including the rex begonia, ferns, and a rhapis palm, which give extra humidity to combat the dry air indoors, the greatest enemy of plants.

72

An inexpensive slab of exposed aggregate forms the cleverly made platform from which water falls in continuous streams. The Featherock (a
manufactured material) used here appears massive but is actually light in
weight. Plants attached to the porous rock grow with little attention in the
moist atmosphere, which is generated by this waterfall.

A waterfall amid pines and azaleas is created from three basins made of exposed aggregate. The water from the lowest reservoir is lifted by means of an inexpensive water pump to the topmost basin and falls from a spout to trickle into the middle receptacle. The pebbled floor is in keeping with the austere setting.

(Left) Featherock is used here to create a rustic effect, with pines and ferns in abundance around a cement deck, cantilevered over the pool. Water gushes in sheets from massive "rocks." The scene, screened by translucent panels, gives an authentic woodsy effect that costs much less than a mountain cabin, and you can stay home weekends.

(Below) Some device is needed to get rid of chlorinated water splashed onto the apron of a pool. Here a trench of gravel covered with hardware cloth serves as a decorative design element and prevents the pebbles from being kicked or thrown into the pool.

(Right) A square of large water-worn river rocks serves to emphasize the weird contortions of the branches of a specimen pyracantha. A few sprouts of bronze ajuga between the rocks removes the sterile effect and enhances the beauty of the pebbles. This low-upkeep, simple garden makes more elaborate plantings seem inept and tasteless.

(Below) Square or irregularly shaped modules serve best for bold plantings near a swimming pool. If these are set into the deck or cement apron on a raised curb, the plants are not damaged by splashing pool water. With decorative boulders a few plants will achieve the same effect as a larger planting. Here a black pine is used as the major element with tufts of spiky blue fescue to serve as accents.

River pebbles seen through the clear water are the basis for this pool's attraction. The plantings of mondo-grass and lily-turf (Liriope) are added niceties and the pine tree bending gracefully gives the entire scene the proper touch.

feather, and primrose creeper, may be used. A single full-sized water-lily must have a container ten inches deep and fifteen inches in diameter, placed at least sixteen inches under water.

There are two basic kinds of water-lilies, the hardy and the tropical. A good lily pond should have some of each, for the hardy lilies start blooming early in the spring but, for the most part, stop flowering in late summer. Tropical lilies start late but continue until the first freeze. When they go dormant they can be stored in moist sand in a frost-free basement until planting time (June 1st).

Night-blooming tropical lilies are an exceptional luxury for those who enjoy their garden after dark. These aristocrats begin to open when the sun goes down and stay open all night; some remain open almost until noon the next morning. They should be purchased each year.

FISH

Another way of adding bright colors to your pool is to stock it with goldfish, or *koi*, fancy members of the carp family. Fanciers stress that they are as different as dogs and cats. The *koi* specialists say *koi* resemble dogs in affection and response, while goldfish are more like cats. It is certain that *koi* are most colorful when viewed from above, while goldfish are most striking, because of their long fins, when seen from the side.

Both are expensive, especially when the larger sizes are desired, and both must be removed to the indoors wherever the pool freezes solid. Certain rare goldfish are too delicate to overwinter even in areas where ice doesn't form.

OTHER ANIMALS FOR THE POOL

Frogs and salamanders add interest but are difficult to confine. Turtles, too, have a habit of wandering away. Tadpoles eat mosquito larvae or any other insect that enters the pool. The best scavengers are snails which feed on decayed vegetation and clean up green algae scum. The largest and hardest working of all snails is the Japanese trap-door snail, although the ram's horn type is also useful and reproduces readily.

Chapter V

PATHS AND FLOORS

Walk on Beauty

No single project can have a more permanent effect on the garden scene than a bit of pebble mosaic, tile patterns, or simple exposed aggregate slabs in the patio floor. If you look around you'll find a place where a more decorative paving would add indispensable color and brightness.

Pebble mosaics were used long before the invasion of the Moors into Spain. They brought the patio concept of gardening to the attention of Europeans and some of the finest examples of their artistry are still to be found in the Moorish gardens. Simple patterns composed of repeated panels are the most effective. Pebbles set on edge rather than flat give a more interesting texture and make patterns that flow dramatically.

Tile designs for garden floors were featured in ancient Greek gardens and some were preserved when volcanic ash covered Pompeii. A colored tile inserted here and there in a bricked patio floor adds life and color all out of proportion to the effort involved. There are

This pebble mosaic was seen in the gardens of the Alhambra in Spain. The design is made by placing darker pebbles on edge while the flat, lighter colored stones are used as the background. This simple method creates a floor that is beautiful and practical.

A simple, rustic way to make a garden path and steps is with logs. If lumber is scarce you may use the boards cut from the outside of the log. These slabs make excellent headers and risers. Trees felled making room for the house on a wooded lot may be utilized to outline paths, to make rustic furniture and garden structures.

Rounds cut from large trees and waterproofed make excellent paths or stepping "stones" in the garden. Placed at intervals along well-traveled trails they prevent damage to grass and groundcover and lend a striking sight.

The more expensive tile are used sparingly in this effective design. Squares of plain cement are set at angles to each other, and interstices filled by tiles made for this purpose. This floor is suitable for any garden style.

A broad area of homogeneous concrete is broken up with great simplicity
by filling the spaces between squares with river stones. Before the cement
hardens the squares are cut out and the smooth cement between removed
with a trowel. Into this space pebbles are pressed firmly and the excess
cement removed with a broom before it hardens.

Slabs of concrete in rectangles are poured, using header boards to shape them. The space between is planted with dichondra. In colder climates, Irish-moss, sea thrift or pinks might be used instead. Woolly thyme is also a hardy substitute for dichondra. Blue fescue in the squares completes the artistic pattern.

88

tiles available to suit every type of garden from the formal to the rustic.

Stepping stones with an imprinted design are among the easiest improvements. Simply dig holes the size and shape desired and fill them with concrete. Any texture or surface treatment (including imprints of leaves) may be used to give them individuality.

Exposed pebbles, crushed rock, roofing gravel, and marble chips are some of the materials that offer interesting textural possibilities. All of these have a homespun quality compatible to any garden. To add these surfaces, simply press pebbles into the soft concrete. They must be pushed or pounded into the concrete so that the cement grips their sides as well as the bottom surface, otherwise they will loosen and come out. Perhaps a better way is to press the material lightly into the surface of fresh concrete and trowel until the stones are covered with cement. Cement comes to the surface when troweled. Then, after the cement has begun to harden, wash the surface with water. Loose mortar can be removed with a brush. Another method of molding concrete is to place the textural material on the bottom of the mold, pour the concrete on top and reverse the product for use. Although the last method seems the easiest, it is tricky and most difficult.

Washing the surface with a ten percent solution of muriatic acid (hydrochloric) five to ten days after the cement has hardened will bring out the quality of the textural material. When blocks are to be moved, make them small enough to be easily handled.

FLAGSTONE AND BRICK FLOORS

Pre-cast slabs, bricks, or flagstones may be set in a bed of sand to make a patio floor and if spaces are left, and mortar is not used between joints, low plants can add a great deal to their beauty. It is best not to create a mowing problem by planting grass. To fill the interstices with a more vibrant foliage color than green, choose among purple ajuga, blue fescue, Scotch-moss, or snow-in-summer. For green more pleasing than grass, use creeping baby's-breath, Irish-moss, or in semitropical areas, dichondra. An added bonus of flowers appears when you choose thrift, pinks, moss phlox, stone-cress, or the annual sweet-alyssum. The latter seeds so readily and grows so quickly that it will spring up year after year without replanting.

Plain cement alternates here with exposed pebble squares. Where a square is left out for design purposes a planting of velvet sedum (Sedum dasy-phyllum) fills in. This creates a more interesting pattern of textures and relieves the monotony of concrete.

A narrow sidewalk is given more impact and more importance by colored squares of concrete. An alternate shortcut is provided by circles of exposed aggregate that prevent an unsightly path across the lawn. The narrow bed adjacent to the garage is filled with big-leaved perennials—bear's-breech (Acanthus) and bergenia, sometimes called Saxifrage.

(Right) The monotony of a solid slab of cement is broken up by geometric patterns filled with washed river stones. The decorative design gives a contrast in textures to heighten the interest.

(Below) Shredded fir bark, called "Walk-on," is used to provide a cushion against skinned knees. This quick-drying material prevents mud and mess in the play yard. Coarser bark is called "Decorative" and comes in various sizes from acorn to chunks the size of tennis balls. It is used as a mulch around permanent plantings.

(Right) Contrasting textures of rock, ajuga and river stones are used in a pleasing design. The stones are separated from the vegetation by a corrugated aluminum strip or curb that is inexpensive and flexible, creating free-flowing patterns for the beds.

(Below) A rock mulch is a good way to beautify a small area that cannot be easily maintained in lawn or groundcover. Here river stones, kept free of weeds by an underlayer of black plastic, serve as a substitute for solid concrete.

A flagstone terrace interplanted with low, ground-hugging plants. If color is desired there are many plants to choose from (see text). If the space between flagstones is left unplanted weeds are sure to thrive there.

A garden path need not be constructed like a sidewalk. For little used paths a few stepping stones suffice. Here, bordered with hyacinths, is a fragrant pathway made of flagstone. The groundcover is mother-of-thousands (Saxifraga stolonifera).

Flagstones set flush with the soil surface are overgrown by a groundcover giving a rustic, natural appearance to this walk through the woods. The irregular shapes, softened by the spreading growth, achieve the desired casual effect. Woolly thyme would be a suitable groundcover for cold winter areas.

NARROW BORDERS

The tendency, if you have a narrow border, is either to neglect it or to fill it with one kind of plant that adapts to the confines of the small space. Of course, grass fills the billing here but it must be mowed and narrow strips give more edging problems than they're worth. Iris is a great favorite because you can plant it and forget it except for the annual six weeks or so when it's in bloom. Then you congratulate yourself for your perspicacity in choosing it. But there are other solutions that can add more color and prolong the blooming period. One choice is to fill the area with loose gravel or brightly colored stones, and plant succulents such as sempervivum and *Sedum spectabile.* The sedum flowers in late summer and autumn—pink, rose, red, or carmine—when flowers are more welcome than when the iris blooms. They need even less attention than iris.

One problem with using gravel is the growth of weeds. These can be controlled with a weedkiller but a better way is to place a sheet of black plastic beneath the gravel. Tarpaper will do as well. Both should be perforated at intervals to allow rain to drain through. Try clusters of larger rocks with lily-turf or daylily nestled in a leeward crevice to decorate your narrow border. This gravelly space will blend with your driveway and contrast nicely with the larger expanses of grass or groundcover.

A narrow border is sufficient for an espalier or vine if there is a wall handy, or it may be planted with low shrubs such as rosemary or flowering quince. In late spring, bedding plants such as petunia or Madagascar periwinkle will relieve with spots of color. In a sunny location a planting of low-growing floribunda roses would give a maximum of color year after year.

Sometimes the best material for the floor of the garden is the shredded bark that is sold in various sizes. The coarsest is often the best because its texture fits into the garden better than the finer grades. Coarsest fir bark with pieces the size of charcoal briquets is the most decorative under shrubs and trees. The acorn size blends well with finer textured lawns, flower beds, and groundcovers. The finest textured, sometimes sold under the brand name, "Walk On" bark, is most used in play areas.

The old tanbark, a stringy fibrous material that is a residue from the leather tanning industry, is generally very scarce but is sometimes available in the immediate vicinity of tanneries.

A *wide entry sidewalk is indented for added interest. It leaves a narrow bed for bulbs and shrubs that do not become overpowering. Tulips and polyantha primroses are used, along with gold-dust plant and camellia. A hardier, big-leaved shrub that would be decorative against the board and batten fence is the bottlebrush buckeye* (Aesculus parviflora).

102

Chapter VI

PRIVATE PATIOS

Outdoor Living Areas and Atriums

If you love plants you can have them in your intimate surroundings by taking advantage of glass walls, windows, and skylights wherever they occur. Plants need light but architects have not until recently designed banks of lamps and indoor sources of light to accommodate plantings.

The newest homes have central skylights with a glass-enclosed plant-growing area directly underneath. This plant room, called an atrium, can grow trees, flowering shrubs, and groundcovers that bloom over long periods. It is easy to select plants to keep the atrium in continuous color. Tropical foliage plants, beautifully marked and variegated, add to the excitement of these gardens.

Floor-level planters have a great advantage in bringing the plants close, so that they are more intimately observed and enjoyed. When they are in pots or containers they assume the dimensions of a picture or work of art that is displayed. However, a raised bed of goodly proportions accommodating several kinds of plants brings the planting

Against a bright living room wall in a home with much glass, an exotic fishtail palm thrives. This palm is too tender to grow outdoors, even in Southern California, but it thrives here amid the other greenery.

PRIVATE PATIOS

103

(Left) The fluted glass in a hallway gives a perfect background for this handsome dracaena from tropical Africa. It grows in the dark jungles and is ideal for dimly lit indoor locations. The three-legged wrought iron support and porous clay container insure fast drainage needed for this plant. Other similar plants that would grow in this location are ti (Cordyline terminalis and C. stricta), and the corn plant, Dracaena fragrans. They may be moved outside against the same glass wall when the weather is mild.

(Below) This house designed for plant lovers Mr. and Mrs. Karl Wagner by architect Cliff May has a garden of tropical plants inside the front door. The floor level planter contains caladiums, dieffenbachia, and dracaena in front of sliding doors reinforced with a bold grillwork.

(Robert C. Cleveland)

(Right) This glass-enclosed patio is large enough to use for dining. You are looking from the living room through the patio, or atrium, into the bedroom. Heavy sliding doors keep the high humidity of the garden room from damaging the furnishings of other rooms and at the same time afford a total view of the growing and flowering plant life.

(Below) The way the indoor and the outdoor extensions of a garden can complement each other is shown in this scene from the motion picture Las Vegas Story. Ferns and philodendron are used against the store wall indoors, while outside, aralia and New Zealand flax are the dominant plants. The use of the same stone in the fireplace wall and in the patio wall, creates a feeling that the room encompasses the whole outdoors. The same inside-outside illusion has been used by many architects in contemporary homes.

(Right) The Karl Wagner's home has an open atrium under a skylight. The plantings of Spathiphyllum 'Mauna Loa' in bloom (white) are surrounded by a rare species of Aglaonema from Malaya, the skeleton-like leaves of aphelandra, and a maranta. From the center post hangs a beautiful columnea, a gesneriad.

(Below) In an indoor dining room, a small pool and waterfall surrounded by Featherock is used for plantings of dracaena (in corner), dieffenbachia, ivy, and philodendron. Plastic flowers float in the pool. Many water plants and fish could be used instead.

(Robert C. Cleveland)

A pecky cypress wall in this glass-ceilinged patio contains a collection of exotic staghorn ferns. Several species shown here come mostly from Australia and the South Seas. They are much sturdier than they look as they are inured to drought and dry air by their epiphytic habit.

back to the proper perspective and scale. In raised beds filled with peat moss, potted plants may be set for long periods during cold weather and taken outdoors in summer without disturbing the tender roots.

Although the word "patio" has a dictionary meaning of an enclosed garden and "private patios" would seem to be redundant, the word has different meanings for different people. The Spanish *patio* originated when walled gardens were the only kinds of garden you could have, because marauding bands of despoilers would invade homes outside the walls of a town. Even inside the town open gardens were prey to anyone and every passerby might help himself to the fruits, vegetables, and flowers grown openly.

The terrace, on the other hand, is an open space adjacent to the house, which is used as an outdoor living area. The word originated when it was found necessary to build up or terrace the land above the foundation so the door to the living area could open directly onto the area, without steps.

There are other terms used in other countries to describe an outdoor living area, such as *lanai* in the South Seas and *loggia* in Italy. The old-fashioned term veranda or portico, had a similar meaning but it was architecturally part of the house. A gazebo is a separate garden structure, preferably with a view, that is open or has glass siding all around it. The teahouse would be a comparable structure in the Japanese garden, while the *engawa* is a narrow deck that provides a transit walk between house and garden.

Today, any extension of the home used for outdoor living is termed a patio, but you can get more genuine pleasure, more fulfillment, out of a patio off your bedroom, bathroom or living room than from any garden you are forced to share with neighbors.

The bathroom patio, no matter how small, creates a luxurious spell that makes you feel that you are bathing alfresco. It also give you a chance to admire the wonders of nature close up and give concentrated attention to details of leaf form and coloration that would ordinarily escape you.

A bedroom patio allows you to enjoy the garden after dark in the comfort of your restful pajamas or robe. It offers a place to share your nightcap with the sounds of the night and the beauty of the stars. It is of greatest importance that your privacy be absolute and your security guaranteed, for nothing less will do.

Bathing too, need not be excluded from a garden scene, and the

(Left) *An elaborate bedroom patio is bedecked with Spanish-moss, tree-trunk bromeliads, and orchids. The large leaves in the center with the holes in them are sometimes called Swiss cheese vine, but it is better known by its scientific name* Monstera. *The arrowhead-shaped leaves belong to a philodendron. On the ground, covered with baby's-tears, is the terrestrial bromeliad,* Cryptanthus, *and to its left the rare* Vriesia hieroglyphica. *In the left foreground is the cycad,* Dion edule, *and in the center, sago palm,* Cycas revoluta.

(Below) *A close-up of the plantings reveals a collection of bromeliads, mostly species of* Tillandsia, *attached to manzanita branches, making a "bromeliad tree," draped with Spanish-moss. In the background amid the rocks are several plants of maidenhair fern and a fine specimen of the cycad* Dion circinalis. *At the extreme left are the richly veined leaves of* Anthurium.

113

A larger bathroom patio is provided with redwood rounds to make a path and a large sliding door to give ready access. The wide overhang gives privacy while the narrow band of open sky allows trees and other plants that need more light to thrive. Lounging and sunbathing, as in the Sonnenbades *of Vienna, is easy to achieve in a garden like this.*

bathroom, like the kitchen, may provide the moist air more healthful to plants than in any other room of the house.

To have this security you must either have a hillside home, where the steep slope of the hill guarantees freedom from prying eyes, or a secure fence. Some would demand that the small patio be roofed in addition, though a lath or lattice roof or screened enclosure should give you enough assurance to enjoy your outdoor extension. A sliding door from the room itself gives easy access to the small patio, but usually an outdoor entrance is needed for the chores of watering and fertilizing. This can be a sturdy gate that blends into the fence so as to be unnoticed.

However, it is the atrium, fully enclosed by the home that offers the continual day to day, hour after hour opportunity to live with plants as they continually change their position toward light, and develop mature flowers and fruit. Glass walls and a skylight provide excellent growing conditions for many plants, both colorful and intriguing. Some source of moisture must usually be provided together with circulation of air. In the absence of air circulation, unless temperatures are kept absolutely even, there will be a condensation of moisture on the glass. With the glass clouded this way, there is less illusion of intimacy. Plants, however, will thrive in a hermetically sealed atmosphere, so it is unnecessary to admit air for the plants to breathe. Plants do not breathe, but they do respire. However, the oxygen released in photosynthesis is more than that necessary for respiration.

This beautiful patio has a wide access door from the outside which facilitates watering but closes tightly (A) to give complete privacy. But a wide sliding window makes it possible to bring the outdoors inside in mild weather (B).

B

(Left) Beside a sunken Roman bath, separated by a glass wall is an enclosed private patio. The dramatic leaves of a monstera and the graceful fronds of a palm, contrast pleasingly. A fern grows in the subdued light on the patio floor.

(Below) In New Orleans an intimate patio off the living room has a spiral stairs to the second-floor balcony. The patio's central accent is a piece of treasured statuary. Huge floor-to-ceiling sliding doors open to embrace the outdoors.

A redwood deck, set flush with the planting bed allows this collection of rex begonias to be viewed close up. Plastic cushions make the watering procedure less troublesome. In the background, one of the more choice indoor plants, a blossoming bromeliad can be seen.

The Japanese-style patio with a pagodalike roof is almost like a teahouse. The huge paper lantern makes it usable after dark. A portable garden in the left foreground has a rare dwarf Atlas cedar with mondo-grass and shore juniper. The two pots at the right contain specimen plants of the weeping banyan.

Chapter VII

THE SHORES

Plants and Flowers Beside
Oceans and Lakes

At the ocean, lakeshore, or wherever the untempered wind blows free, sturdy plants are needed to survive the continual buffeting. Every homeowner who has an air conditioner finds that plants close to it suffer from the constant breeze. A deflector to shunt the force of the cold blast away from plants will preserve their beauty without the necessity of moving them. The deflector usually may be pointed upward without effecting plants but sometimes it is necessary to use a cloth or crimped steel sheet, such as that used for metal lath, to take the sting out of the wind.

Many plants are adapted by nature to endure such onslaughts but unless you know their native region you would never suspect that they have this quality. Along the broad shores of the United States you will find native trees such as the Monterey cypress, red-cedar, spruce, sea-grape, and willow. But we must go abroad, especially to the

This tree is a myoporum from New Zealand. Acacias and eucalyptus, the olive, hopbush, and New Zealand Christmas tree are used in California. The beefwood, sassafras, silk tree (Albizia julibrissin) are favorites of the South, tupelo and southern magnolia are used in Florida. On the Atlantic Coast, the pea tree or caragana, hawthorn, oak, honey locust, Russian olive, ash, and elm are favored.

THE SHORES

Annuals as a group do well in the first zone of exposure, but some thrive better there than anywhere else. The most beautiful gaillardias are seen on Cape Cod, and rose-moss can be grown right down to the tide line. Here snapdragon (A) and stock (B) grow luxuriant on an oceanic coast.

A

Perennials that thrive in the dazzling sunshine and cool breezes at the ocean include statice (A), Pride of Madeira or echium (B), Shasta daisy and other chrysanthemums (C), lavender, campanulas, daylily, Coreopsis maritima, 'Silvermound' artemisia, lily-turf, and geraniums (D).

A B

C D

Groundcovers that accommodate to saline soil and driven spray include sea thrift (shown here), beach strawberry, bearberry, ice plants, mondograss, sedums and sempervivums, dusty miller, Natal-plum, cotoneaster, lantana, prostrate rosemary, Serbian bellflower, pinks, ivy geranium, thyme, periwinkle, and Koreangrass.

128   *A*   *B*

Some shrubs that can weather the storms at the beach are the bottlebrush or melaleuca from New Zealand (A), pittosporums, India hawthorn (B), veronica or hebe (C), escallonia, and Scotch broom, all used extensively on the West Coast. Sea-grape, euonymus, and oleander are common in Florida, while rock-rose, heathers, tamarisk, sumac, buckthorn, viburnums, and snowberry are found on the East Coast.

C

Pines and all needle evergreens are excellent choices for planting near the ocean and wherever the wind is severe. Shore juniper is a prostrate form that is adapted to saline soils and beach conditions. In Florida and California, the star pine is commonly seen at the shore and Monterey cypress is a trademark in California, especially near Carmel. Spruce, fir, and cedar rival pines on the Eastern seaboard.

130

islands of the world, to find the great majority of plants that have built-in wind resistance: Japanese black pine, Scotch pine, English hawthorn, casuarina and eucalyptus from Australia, the holly oak and tamarisk from the Mediterranean. From the windy steppes of Siberia comes the Russian olive.

While trees afford the first line of defense against wind, there are several things that can be done to soften the gales before they reach your property. Sand dunes are a natural protection that may be induced to form where you want them, by the use of a snow fence. As the sand piles up, this gets the dune started and it will build naturally afterward. The tendency is to grade a shore lot down toward the ocean but this is against the better interests of plant growing. It is surprising what a low grade, tipped toward the ocean will do to temper winds. The top of the rise need not be higher than the base of your windows, so as not to interfere with the precious view, but if it is near enough to the house it will protect all kinds of flowering shrubs and perennials that cannot ordinarily survive in the first zone of exposure. Near the shore is an ideal spot for a sunken garden for this reason.

Sometimes a baffled fence will control the wind better than a solid one, which creates currents that strengthen the force. Baffles can be set so that the view is not limited but the speed of the wind is lowered. On the Pacific Coast transparent plastic or glass panels are used to make walls. The wall need not be composed entirely of these panels but if they are used at intervals they are equally effective.

It is not the force of the wind alone that shapes plants near the seashore to look as though they were molded by the wind. Experiments conducted at the University of Minnesota have shown that it is the sand particles driven by the wind that blast the buds on the windward side and force the plant to grow to the leeward.

As to what flowering plants withstand the harsh conditions near the seashore, consider all annuals (if protected) as good choices. Some that thrive especially well in bright sunshine are snapdragons, gaillardia, celosia, annual chrysanthemum, petunia, everlastings, nasturtium, statice, and zinnia. Cosmos, marigold, rose-moss, verbena, coreopsis, lupines, poppies, bachelor's-button, also grow with vigor and bloom vivaciously.

Perennials that flourish in the glaring sun and salt spray are all those with white or silvery foliage: Silver-king artemisia, dusty miller, beach wormwood, lavender, lamb's-ears, santolina, *Helichrysum petio-*

Roses can be grown in the first zone of exposure but do much better where a protecting wall or fence, such as the one shown here, offers shelter from the fierce winds. The rugosa rose and its hybrids has few rivals as a seashore shrub.

To prevent erosion of his shale cliff, this homeowner built a steel and concrete platform. The edge of the structure makes a planting box for deep-
rooted trees and shrubs, which, when fully grown, will provide shelter.
Erosion by ocean waves is one of the greatest hazards of ocean-front
homes.

133

Redwood boards in a zigzag fashion make a serrated margin for this bed by the sea. It contains tower of jewels echium and other species inured to the first zone of exposure.

latum, sea-holly, saltbush, bush morning-glory, blue fescue, snow-in-summer, pigeon's beak, rock-cress, woolly thyme, and woolly yarrow. Sea thrift, plumbago, coreopsis, iris, daylily, lily-turf, ivy geranium, and *Wedelia trilobata* are also well adapted to the first zone of exposure.

Shrubs that do well include the heathers, heaths, all kinds of roses, rosemary, brooms, beach plum, the shrubby cinquefoils, cotoneasters, rock-rose, pyracantha, junipers, Mugho pine, hypericum, Natal-plum, various viburnums, oleander, several species of *Pittosporum*, and mirror plant (*Coprosma*). In California shrubs from New Zealand called *Griselinia* and *Myoporum* are favorites. India hawthorn, *Melaleuca* (bottlebrush), and *Hebe* (veronica) are also used. For tall windbreaks choose among goat willow, buckthorn, sumac, sea-buckthorn, salt tree, shadbush, rose-of-Sharon, and privet.

Shallow sandy soil, saline water, saltspray, and, where it is a factor, the tide, have an important effect on plant roots. It is not by accident that beachgrass, bayberry, beach plum, wild blueberries, and bearberry are the denizens of our shoreline. The best guide for the newcomer as to what to plant are the successful plantings in the area. A few hours spent on a survey on a Saturday afternoon, with frequent stops to inquire of other homeowners tending to their garden chores, will be of more help than all of the books written on the subject.

To hasten nature's measured stabilization of sand dunes the first procedure is to use a mulch. Any organic material in abundant supply in the area, such as marsh grass, salt hay, wood chips, straw, or ground bark, is excellent. At the seashore, grass clippings, fallen leaves, weeds that haven't gone to seed, and old sod, are too valuable to discard and should be put on a compost pile along with all vegetable trimmings—from corn husks to carrot tops. Avoid adding protein materials such as meat or fish, which create odors and fly problems. Soil is the best source of the microorganisms which will break down the compost, and thin layers of soil, together with added moisture and good air circulation will aid in rapid decomposition.

Sowing ryegrass is a temporary measure for quick protection from blowing sand. Seeds will germinate within three days when temperatures are favorable. But to get permanent stabilization, it is best to plant beachgrass. It spreads by underground runners. The tough leaves are able to grow through deposited sand so that the dune continues to build after the beachgrass is planted.

Epidendrum orchids grow outdoors in Hawaii, sheltered by a wooden fence decorated with bamboo.

Root divisions are preferable to seeding but unless the sprigs are kept moist, there will be erratic growth. Clumps may be obtained from areas where the grass is already established by pulling, shaking free of sand, and separating the crown with two or three erect stems per division. Cut back the top growth and keep the divisions from drying out until planted by wrapping in wet burlap or covering with polyethylene in the shade. Plant one and a half feet apart, about eight inches deep.

Chapter VIII

ROCK GARDENS

Planting with Pebbles, Boulders, and Stones

You may think that desert gardens and alpine gardens have nothing in common except rocks, but that isn't true. Many desert plants are drought-escaping—that is, they live and bloom during the short time when it rains and moisture is available, just like those on the mountaintop. Some are adapted to store water over long periods of drought. These we call succulents and they are found wherever water is in short supply—in the desert or in the mountains where the water is not available to plants because it is frozen into ice.

When we think of the desert it immediately calls cacti to mind, yet there are many deserts of the world where cacti are unknown. Actually cacti are native only to the Americas; deserts of Asia, Africa, and Australia are inhabited by succulents other than the *Cactaceae*, which, nevertheless, is the largest family of succulents.

Alpine plants, including many succulents, just like desert plants, need quick drainage and a natural slope or the banks of a ravine is ideal. Unfortunately, there are few such locations in the average gar-

Pine, juniper, and spruce grow amid boulders of Featherock; each one weighs less than one hundred pounds. They can be moved easily with a hand truck. Blue fescue is used as a border plant along the tree rounds.

ROCK GARDENS

139

One of the most beautiful of all rock-garden plants is Ramonda myconi, *a relative of the popular house plant, the African violet. It comes from the Pyrénées and is hardy well below zero. The broad, scalloped leaves have a rough texture, forming a flat rosette from which the flowering stem arises. The lilac-colored flowers appear in clusters in the month of May. It grows in acid soil, which should have plenty of humus, and thrives best in a crevice of a wall in the cool shade. Ramonda, like the African violet, can be propagated by leaf cuttings.*

An alpine form of the pussy willow is a dwarf plant, easy to grow in the rock garden. In the spring the female flowers resembling soft cat fur, stand erect on leafless branches.

A bluebell from the Carpathian Mountains of Europe thrives in the rock garden. It is not as invasive as many of the species of Campanula used as groundcovers, but is equally tough. The erect flowers are blue and they are held well above the toothed leaves.

den. That is why the traditional rock garden, as such, has had its day, but rocks as a background for plants or used to complement a planting arrangement are often useful in the garden. A garden without rocks is a mere flower bed, ideal for masses of colorful plants but not to show off the beauty of the individual plant.

There are many stones that might be pretty in a collection but these do not serve in a rock garden. For instance, those usually selected by the "rock hound" are not suited. Rocks should be rough and angular, with much character. They should be of unobtrusive color. If you choose limestone, it should be used exclusively, and the same is true of tufa, a porous volcanic rock. Whatever kind of rock is chosen, it should all be of the same kind, the same texture, and the same color. If stratified sedimentary rock rather than igneous is chosen, the layers should all run in the same plane, not in haphazard fashion. You should choose the right-sized stone for the location with the same care you would choose the plant, for in effect, you are making a permanent arrangement that will either please or offend as long as it exists. Never scatter stone around; this gives a cluttered look. At least one-third of each rock should be buried to give a more stable appearance. Avoid regular spacing between rocks. Where many small rocks are available and no large ones, cluster them in a natural effect.

If you live in the Southwest, a desert garden is not a difficult accomplishment. All you have to do is utilize the plants that will grow naturally in arid conditions. Elsewhere they require certain measures to accommodate them outside their natural habitat.

The most important cultural requirement for desert plants is sharp drainage and this is most easily accomplished by building a mound. If space is limited, a raised bed or container will serve.

Many of the contemporary low-maintenance landscapes in the West are combinations of rock-and-desert plantings that form the latest concept of the rock garden. The desert garden decorated with wagon wheels and skulls is a thing of the past. The modern desert landscape will have crushed rock of various hues forming a pattern in the lawn and with groupings of low desert plants combined with taller vertical accents planted in locations around the yard.

Desert gardens should never depend solely on cacti, although a few well chosen specimens add interest and design elements to any desert garden. Trees such as the taller yuccas, Russian olive, pine, aspen, and tamarix, provide vertical accents. Barberry, juniper, lan-

(Right) Woolly thyme will invade the entire garden if given a start. As a soft gray cover for rocks and bare soil, it is unexcelled but it is generally not hardy below ten degrees above. It can be slowed down by confining to a rock crevice. Good between stepping stones.

(Below) Golden thyme serves a double use—as a culinary herb and as a star in the rock garden. With gold-edged leaves and the tiny lavender flowers, it is so sturdy that it is often the last plant that survives in old abandoned gardens. This species is hardy to about zero.

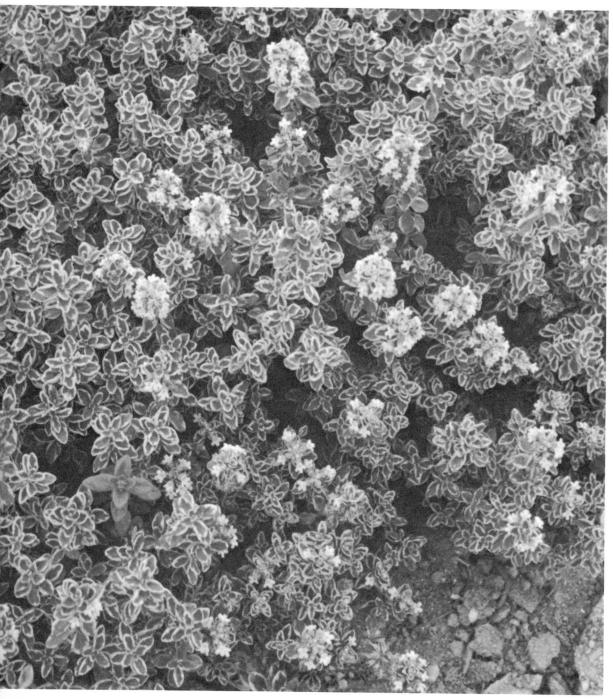

144

Stone-cress, Aubrieta deltoidea, *is a common denizen of rock gardens, but it often spreads too vigorously. Gray-green leaves and rose to dark red or lilac flowers appear in spring. It grows well in full sun if given plenty of water and is hardy below zero.*

A rectangular bed indented in a brick sidewalk holds a collection of succulents. The vertical accent is a barrel cactus, while the toothed leaves
behind it belong to agave. Scattered about are species of Echeveria.

This is a particularly handsome species of houseleek, familiarly known as hen-and-chickens. The leaves are tipped with reddish-brown points. One of the hardiest of all succulents, it withstands twenty degrees below zero. Starry reddish flowers are produced in clusters in spring. Sempervivum species grow slowly but they are among the toughest rock-garden plants.

The base of a rock wall, in its reflected heat, is an ideal location for patterns of succulents in a modular design. Here are two species of Echeveria growing in gravel beds.

150

(Left) Two specimens of a columnar cactus known as Cereus peruvianus *display the common ribbed form and the deformed 'Monstrosus' variety, knotted and gnarled. Both succumb to hard frost and must be brought inside in winter in the cold areas. A barrel cactus (foreground), and a prickly-pear complete this desert planting.*

(Below) This desert landscape in Palm Springs, California, features ocotillo (left) and yucca (right) as vertical elements, while petunias and juniper give balance and color.

A desert garden features yucca (extreme right) and saguaro cactus (near front door), two clumps of a rare species of Agave *and a prickly-pear. In the foreground (left) is a chollo cactus and extreme left an ocotillo. The space between the plants is covered with fine pebbles.*

tana, Texas ranger (*Leucophyllum*), privet, rosemary, santolina, and germander are good shrubs to mingle with prickly-pear or barrel cactus. Agave, palms, oleander, and ocotillo are limited to the warmer areas.

Groundcovers for a desert garden may be chosen from these: prostrate juniper, blue fescue, dusty miller, woolly thyme, prostrate rosemary. Succulents such as sedums, sempervivums, and rose-moss may be used anywhere in the country.

Raised beds are generally limited in size so that only a single accent plant is used but in a long bed several specimens might be planted as well as a low spilly groundcover. The forms should be varied for greater interest. In a container that may be moved indoors or to a heated garage or basement, a columnar cactus might be combined with a barrel type. Echeveria might be used as a low accent.

In warm, wet areas desert plants can be grown by limiting the amount of moisture the soil receives with the aid of a huge sheet of plastic (polyethylene) film. This is placed on top of the ground or under a layer of colored gravel.

You do not have to build a mound to have a rock garden. A natural slope can be utilized with terraces. Select the background carefully so that the desolate beauty and stark lines of cacti and other succulents are delineated. A hot, sunny corner against a wood or concrete block fence is ideal.

The outline of the garden should not be geometric but composed of natural curves. Make it narrow enough so there is easy access for weeding and growing. Cacti are bad customers when you have to move among them or bend down in their vicinity. Make the beds accessible from one side only, a maximum of three feet wide, and double that if they can be reached from two sides. If wider beds are required, use walks or stepping stone paths through the widest area.

If you have difficulty in finding large enough rocks in your locality, you may wish to consider lightweight volcanic rock called "Featherock," or one of the fiber-glass imitation rocks used by moviemakers. The latter, in various shades and shapes, looks like granite boulders. In some types, the color does not fade in the sun. The hollow forms are very lightweight and have a natural appearance, being cast from actual rocks.

Featherock has a great advantage in that it may be painted and glued together to form monoliths, which may be carved to appear as a

(Left) A fiber-glass rock looks very natural amid the ajuga. The mold for the fiber-glass was made from a real rock selected for its interesting character. Behind the rock is an espaliered podocarpus, which is not hardy.

(Below) Featherock has the quality of holding moisture in its porous matrix. Plants grow readily in pockets filled with planter mix. Here two fancy-leaved geraniums decorate a striated gray Featherock that looks heavy but weighs just over fifty pounds.

155

An outcropping of rock was created from matched pieces of Featherock fitted together in a natural way to make an interesting feature on this bare hillside. The double waterfall and hidden pools are part of a recirculating system that utilizes a submerged water pump.

single outcropping. The rocks are so light that a large three-by-five-feet boulder weighs only about four-hundred pounds. As the surface is sharp, gloves must be worn when handling to prevent your hands from being shredded.

Sand or gravelly soil should always be used in constructing a rock garden. For desert plants, no organic matter should be added. For alpines twenty-five percent peat or other composted organic matter is used to make the soil acid. Desert plants thrive in neutral or slightly alkaline soil, so lime may be needed where soil is naturally acid.

Chapter IX

MOUNDS

Make Your Level Garden
More Interesting

The newest thing in landscaping is the use of earth as a means of enclosure. A man-made mound of soil that transforms a flat spot into a rolling hill has several important advantages, though this method is not open to everyone. A built-up slope should not be steeper than one foot of rise in two feet of ground. This means that a ridge only four feet high must be at least sixteen feet wide. Such a hillock may be too space-consuming in your garden. With retaining walls, however, the width could be reduced considerably. Retaining walls are expensive and you will probably not want to consider a mound unless you have at least a sixteen-foot width in which to work.

HOW TO BUILD A MOUND

A mound is simply a pile of earth, usually with a central core of coarse gravel to expedite drainage. Do not excavate under the mound; to pro-

A mound garden covered with iceplant and gazania has a cotoneaster and heavenly-bamboo (center) to add interest.

vide perfect drainage, it should rest on the old soil surface. The size and shape may be varied to fit the location.

Where you put the mound in relation to its surroundings is of utmost importance. A full sun position is best but it must fit into the landscape. Do not place it in the middle of the lawn like a desert island. The edge of the lawn or a secluded corner of the property are good locations.

After you select the site and determine how high you want it, the outline of the mound can be drawn on the soil. Use loose soil on a lawn area to mark the dimensions. A hose is a good device to make graceful curves of a free-form design that is much more interesting and more natural than an angular shape.

For the base, any coarse, porous material such as crushed rock, broken bricks, or concrete rubble may be used, but gravel is easily available and very suitable. A three- to six-inch layer is then covered with the same amount of builder's sand and shaped roughly. The remainder is of good garden topsoil or any soil enriched with a composted humus in the proportion of ten percent humus and ninety percent soil. The center should not be a sharp ridge but a gradual slope to a rounded top, tapered into gullies and curved contours. Use a rake to shape and smooth the surface and water it well to settle and firm the soil. Avoid steep slopes that will wash and create problems.

If you have fill soil from any excavation such as a pool, basement, or just footings for foundations or cement walks or driveways, it is considerably less expensive to build a mound with the excess soil than it is to haul it away. To accommodate a large quantity of soil you may make the ridge higher or longer or build a dry wall at the lot lines and have the gradual slope oriented toward the house. A mound is also the answer to your problem if garden soil is too heavy and lacks sufficient drainage for trees and shrubs to grow. Then the level soil surface becomes the drainage base and the soil on the mound drains equally well in all directions.

The greatest advantage of a mound is for noise control. Although plants have some effect in depressing sound waves, a low mound will deaden noises that originate at the pavement level. For homes adjacent to busy streets where the whir of tires and the screech of brakes are a constant annoyance, mounds serve as an excellent barrier. If the street is depressed below the level of the house, the embankment will

Hiding the ugly fireplug is the chief purpose of this mound on which a variety of groundcovers have been used. Iceplant is around the standpipe with santolina (right), dusty miller (behind), and rosemary (left). They have wisely chosen to hide the fireplug from the house rather than from the street, which would probably violate fire regulations.

deaden obnoxious sounds but if it is elevated the only solution is a mound and plantings.

Heavily foliaged trees such as pine and spruce do much to reduce high-pitched noises but do little to diminish low rumblings and the roar of engines. A recent study at the Missouri Botanical Garden indicates that plantings twenty-five to fifty feet wide reduce noise at the higher frequencies of ten to twenty decibels by more than half. The lowest frequencies, the most difficult to muffle by plantings, are generally less annoying. Size and density of plantings are critical in noise control and narrow hedges are relatively ineffective.

Because plants that require sharp drainage are the best candidates for slope plantings, the mound can be used for a rock, alpine, or desert garden. To make the mound serve as a taller screen you may wish to plant trees or tall shrubs. A rolling grass lawn is an excellent choice for covering a mound. But because of the difficulty in mowing, watering, and fertilizing grass on a slope, most mounds are covered with patterns of drought-resistant groundcovers.

Best candidates for plantings include many plants with eye-pleasing color either in flowers or foliage. Those with colorful foliage offer more permanent patterns and include purple, red or bronze; white, silver-gray or blue-green, and yellow or gold. Red or bronze foliage is rather rare among hardy plants and ajuga in selected varieties is about the only perennial available. The basil, 'Dark Opal,' can be used for temporary color. Snow-in-summer is the most dependable of those with whitish foliage. Dusty miller, blue fescue, woolly thyme, woolly yarrow, wormwood, 'Silvermound' artemisia, and lavender-cotton are other good choices. Scotch-moss, gold crown-vetch, golden dead nettle (*Lamium galeobdolon*), and 'Gold Feather' feverfew are useful for furnishing yellow foliage.

Among the sedums, sempervivums and other succulents are many good plants for mounds. In semitropical areas the vivid flowers of iceplant are excellent, as well as gazania and ivy geranium. The best hardy flowering groundcovers include phlox, strawberry, fleabane, perennial coreopsis, basket-of-gold, rock-cress, and perennial candytuft. St. John's-wort, sun-rose, and lantana are often used.

Chapter X

PORTABLE GARDENS

**Transform a Drab or Barren Spot
Indoors and Out**

Gardening in containers is much more interesting, far more challenging, and the results are more dramatic when more than one species is used in a single planter. These can be appropriately called spot gardens (as well as groups of separate pots) and their composition requires plant know-how as well as artistic talent. Only plants that have the same requirements in soil, sunlight, and water may be used.

Some compatible plants that need little water, full sun and light, and sandy soil, are ocotillo, *Agave attenuata*, aloe, sedum, and aeonium. These make a pleasing combination for a container on a hot, sunlit patio.

Another attractive combination, one that needs plenty of water and even withstands flooding, contains Egyptian papyrus, umbrella-palm (*Cyperus alternifolius*), and mondo-grass (*Ophiopogon japonicus*). These thrive in heavily organic soil, rich in fertilizer elements, and full sun for best growth.

Here is an arrangement of potted plants that would make an eyecatching ornament in any garden. The plant, a succulent called elephant plant (Portulacaria afra), grows well indoors or out but it is tender to frost. It is so-called because it is said to be eaten by elephants.

(Right) A handsome specimen of dracaena with variegated leaves is an outstandingly beautiful decoration in any home. The plant requires very little light. It may be used as an indoor-outdoor plant in any area. The planter is from Architectural Pottery.

(Below) This stylish patio is dressed with plants in many shapes in white pottery of all sizes.

166

(Left) Of all the species and varieties of Chinese evergreen, this Aglao-nema pseudobracteata, *is most beautiful, rivaling the flamboyant dieffen-bachias.*

(Below) Best of the indoor orchids are the species of Miltonia. *The flowers last for months in the subdued lights of indoors. When out of bloom it can be content outdoors during the summer months.*

To grace a shaded spot with a suitable container planting, nandina or yew pine might be chosen for a vertical element, aralia for its contrasting bold leaf pattern, with strawberry-begonia as a groundcover. For a container in part sun, choose bamboo with leaves removed except for tufts at the ends of branches, *Mahonia lomariifolia* or *M. bealei* (holly-grape) for its beautiful leaf form, and juniper as a cascading groundcover.

There are two kinds of planters: movable and stationary. And the choice of plant depends on the type of container. For a movable planter you can choose a plant with a period of bloom that is short but glorious, however, for a container fixed in one place, the plant must be good-looking at all times. A long period of bloom, while not essential, is desirable.

Generally the larger the stationary planter, the better, because combinations of plants make a more pleasing design than any single plant. Movable planters must be light to be easily lifted or wheeled out of sight when the bloom is finished. To keep them light, use a planter mix containing perlite, and before you move them let them dry out (a gallon of water weighs ten pounds).

The advantages of portable gardens are many but the greatest is that they end up where you want them. This makes them much more valuable than plants permanently situated. Instead of having to go where they are located to see them, portable plants in effect come to you. They are brought in front and center when they are in spectacular bloom and relegated to an inconspicuous corner when less beautiful. You can have a succession of bloom close at hand if you manage your container gardens successfully.

Portable gardens make indoor-outdoor accommodation practical. Many tropical plants susceptible to frost-damage thrive outdoors in spring, summer, and fall between the first and last frost date and can be moved indoors for the winter. An example is dwarf citrus—orange, lemon, or lime trees—that grow well in a container and accept the reduced light indoors without damage. Other examples are the gardenia 'Mystery,' camellia, tree philodendron, fuchsia, dieffenbachia, some orchids, bromeliads, jade tree, heavenly-bamboo, and many others. If you have a bright picture window or sun room the number of plants you can grow this way is too long to list but includes hibiscus, bougainvillea, bird-of-paradise, and most orchids.

The most exciting indoor plants that adapt to this indoor-outdoor

Star jasmine pruned to grow upright makes an outstanding specimen in a wooden planter. Its delicious fragrance is an added bonus when the plant is in bloom. Hardy to twenty degrees, it can be moved indoors in colder weather.

171

Succulents are adapted by nature to growing in containers. This exotic specimen Kalanchoe beharensis with felty three-cornered leaves is tender to cold but withstands sun and heat outdoors as well as the darkness of our homes.

Sago palm, Cycas revoluta, *is an ideal indoor-outdoor plant because it can survive with good light indoors about six months out of the year. Outdoors it will survive down to twenty degrees, but needs protection from lower temperatures. Cycads are sturdy plants that have survived millions of years (since the Coal Age) on this earth, so don't coddle them.*

A collection of succulents in a metal basin is set off by black pebbles. This will grow anywhere without special care and is a great conversation piece indoors in wintertime.

174

existence are the trees that are coming into vogue now. Foliage that is held above eye level confers a mood indoors that cannot be equalled by flowers and foliage at your feet.

As decorators seek more and more dramatic effects from interior designs they are turning to tall plants—trees—to create the desired sensation. Vertical accents not only lift the spirit upward but produce the impression of being enveloped by the environment. This deep feeling of the security offered by vegetation is perceived not only by the most sensitive but also by the most callous individual.

Towering arches and two-story windows are man-made ways to lift our eyes upward but trees are nature's way of doing so, enfolding the spirit in beauty.

It was the advent of the two-story window and the atrium that opened up homes architecturally to the use of indoor trees and horti-culturalists have been quick to provide suitable specimens. To survive in the reduced light, high temperatures, and low humidity of the modern home, required a search of warm, dry areas all over the world.

These are the requirements for plants living indoors: first of all, trees must be evergreen. Permanence necessitates that the leaves must stay on for several years and be replaced gradually, not in a single flush of growth. Such plants must also have clean habits—not dropping leaves, twigs, sheaths or branches that would produce constant litter. Next the leaves must not only be beautiful but leathery and covered with wax to give a glossy shine. This is the plant's built-in way to reduce damage from drought, especially from low humidity.

One would never dream that indoors the relative humidity is often well below the average for a desert, but this is what happens when we heat our houses. Outdoors the humidity on an average winter day might be fifty percent, ideal for most plants, but the temperature a cold thirty degrees or less. When we take that air indoors and heat it, the relative humidity is lowered drastically. A volume of air—a roomful for instance—contains a fixed amount of water vapor. When the temperature is raised to seventy degrees the amount of water remains exactly the same but the relative humidity will drop to thirty percent, which is too low for all but desert plants. Often in our super-heated homes the relative humidity goes below ten percent—the average humidity on a July day at noon in Death Valley.

A third requirement is the ability to adapt to reduced light conditions indoors. Even in an atrium with a skylight the intensity of light

(Left) Several species of Echeveria *are collected in this interesting iron planter. In the center is a sedum* (S. guatemalense).

(Below) Succulents are ideal for hanging baskets indoors and outdoors, especially this species of Sedum, S. morganianum, *which is not hardy.*

A Japanese barrel holds a fine specimen of the jade plant (Crassula argentea) *commonly grown as a house plant throughout the country. The leaves will be set more closely together if you grow it outdoors in the summer months.*

is well below that outdoors even on a fairly overcast day. If you have a photographic light meter, you can readily see how quickly light diminishes as you move away from a bright window. Even with maximum light indoors, only plants adapted to growing in the shade will be able to survive.

Each of these needed characteristics eliminates plants native to vast areas of the earth, but one family of plants meets most of these demands. This is the Fig Family—of world-wide distribution in the tropics. At first the India rubber, *Ficus elastica*, was utilized and many more beautiful varieties of this favorite were developed. One such plant, called 'Decora,' had larger, much broader leaves with depressed veins that gave the glossy dark green leaf much character. A variegated variety of *F. elastica*, called *doescheri*, first grown in New Orleans, has leaves spotted and dappled with gray, white and cream yellow blotches on a dark green background.

Another popular indoor fig is *Ficus lyrata*, native to tropical Africa, and called the fiddle-leaved fig for good reason. Huge leathery leaves are up to fifteen inches long and deeply indented on the sides like a fiddle (more in scale with a bass viol). The giant leaves are criss-crossed with deep veins which give it a corrugated texture. Other species sometimes used indoors include *F. retusa*, which is the Indian-laurel, *F. r. nitida*, and *F. benjamina*, the weeping banyan of Malaya.

All of these are large trees that in their native lands grow to fifty feet or more tall but can easily be kept down to ceiling height indoors. Their big advantage is their extreme vigor under conditions of stress such as encountered in our homes. All need the same kind of care. Although outdoors they thrive in full sunlight, the tender leaves formed indoors are burned by direct sun. On the other hand too little light will cause them to cast their leaves. The best location is close to a window but out of the streaming sunshine.

The next most useful group of trees for indoor use belong to the *Araliaceae*. One of the most popular is schefflera, known in its native land, Australia, as the Queensland umbrella tree. The best known member of this family is true ivy (*Hedera*), which can be grown in tree form by rooting the upright flower-bearing shoots. Especially handsome is the variegated Algerian ivy (*Hedera canariensis variegata*), which in erect form is known as the ghost tree.

Schefflera is the common name for *Brassaia*, but in the trade it is almost always known as schefflera. *B. actinophylla* has huge seven to

180

*(Left) Australian umbrella tree or schefflera is combined with two philo-
dendrons, kangaroo vine, and sansevieria in a round tub planter. The tree
will grow quickly, especially if it is taken outdoors in the warm months.*

*(Below) Geraniums are ideal for containers but if you combine several
plants you make a more dramatic statement than with a single plant. This
cement planter is heavy and permanent, but breakable if the moist soil is
frozen. Cuttings from the geraniums can be taken and rooted in winter
for setting out in spring.*

The cut-leaved Japanese maple growing in an unusual pottery planter is a decoration for the patio that never ceases to be interesting. As it leafs out, it heralds the spring season. In leaf it blesses the summer months and in autumn the leaves turn red and yellow before they fall. In winter its bare branches look black against the snow.

sixteen palmately parted leaflets in each leaf that may attain two feet in diameter. It grows rapidly in rich soil if given plenty of light, water, and fertilizer but will retain its good looks almost indefinitely indoors in subdued light. True species of *Schefflera* which come from China (*S. delavayi*) and New Zealand (*S. digitata*), are less common but equally satisfactory and easy to grow. A plant often confused with *Schefflera* and *Brassaia* but with a distinct lax or viney habit, is *Tupidanthus calyptratus*, which has no common name. It grows better in less light, being adapted to life on the floor of the jungles in Burma.

Less well known genera of the same family are *Cussonia* from South Africa, *Oreopanax* from Mexico, *Neopanax* and *Pseudopanax* from New Zealand. There are several species of each genus but the one with the most beautiful leaves, which resemble snowflakes, is *Cussonia spicata*. *Oreopanax peltatus*, with leaves something like those of papaya, is called wild papaya in Mexico.

The snowflake aralia is *Trevesia palmata* which comes from south China (Yunnan). Its leaves are cut in an intricate pattern duplicated only by the most complex snowflakes. A popular tropical shade plant often used as a hedge in Acapulco, Hawaii, and Jamaica is *Polyscias* which comes from the South Seas. It is a leafy tree or tall shrub with lacy bipinnate leaves. The variegated type, used most frequently, will reach the ceiling in the average room.

All these members of the *Araliaceae* thrive in the light shade in their native countries and are thus well adapted to growth indoors. All have leathery leaves but need much moisture and good drainage.

The only conifers (needle evergreens) adapted for use indoors are the Norfolk Island pine (also called the star pine), *Araucaria excelsa*, and the Dammar pine, *Agathis robusta*. The first is much more common but you must buy cutting-grown plants rather than seedlings to get a perfect form. The seedlings are very lax and do not produce the beautiful branch patterns of the cuttings.

Although they are not considered trees by the botanist, palms and dracaenas attain the height necessary for the classification. Best palms for indoor use are those that grow naturally in shade, such as the bamboo or lady palms, the sturdy kentia and the parlor palms which have been used for years indoors. The kentia palm is a native of Lord Howe's Island near Australia and is popularly called paradise palm. The outstanding keeping qualities of this plant have endeared it to florists, hotel keepers, and funeral directors all over the world.

186

A dwarf Mugho pine in a weathered container withstands any amount of cold, but not normal house temperatures. The container will break if it's allowed to fill with melted snow or rain and then freeze.

The lady palm, *Rhapis*, is native to South China and grows in graceful clumps with slender bamboolike stems. It is widely used in the orient as a potted palm and is becoming more common here. The parlor palm, *Chamaedorea*, from Mexico, grows only to eight feet and is easy to maintain in dark locations.

Vertical accents are also possible with the many kinds of *Dracaena*, which attain tree heights. These belong to the Lily Family and are found in the tropics all over the world. The closely related genus *Cordyline* to which the *Dracaena indivisa* of the florists belongs, is also used indoors. The "ti" plant of Hawaii, *Cordyline terminalis*, grows twelve feet high and is palmlike in appearance.

Plants in hanging baskets solve the problem of overhead decoration where floor or ground space is limited. But don't hang them where dripping water will ruin the floor or stain the cement, because overwatering is the main secret in growing container plants successfully.

It goes without saying that hanging baskets must be provided with good drainage. You cannot grow many plants in closed containers. Once a month plants should be watered heavily so that the water courses through the planter mix and cascades down through the drainage holes. Then apply a fertilizer, preferably one that is organic or a slow-release product to provide continuous mild nutrition. The planter mix should be a coarse organic material which wets easily and holds water well to keep watering to a minimum.

Some of the best plants for a hanging garden are ivy geranium, rabbit's-foot fern, burro tail, periwinkle, and wandering Jew.

There is hardly a garden that does not utilize an urn, vase, tub, bowl, barrel, or hanging basket to add interest and excitement to the garden. But there are places where the soil is so poor, where drainage is lacking, or tree roots so invasive (sometimes all three together), that the only way to grow deep rooted plants is in containers. Then, too, there are decks, flagstone terraces, and cement or brick patios where containers figure prominently.

Containers may be made of wood, metal, concrete, terra cotta, plastic, ceramic, or glass. When you choose a planter, buy the plant at the same time or have the size well in mind—it is essential that they be in scale. The type of container, its texture, style, and color are important to the best display of a plant.

Verdant vegetation collects dust and the oily film that emanates from the kitchen stove and furnace is, of course, unknown in nature.

188 *The columnar form of this species of Podocarpus, called yew pine, is resistant to cold down to twenty degrees. This interesting planter is of wood.*

Palm trees, especially this lady palm, are excellent house plants because 189
they naturally grow in the shade. The Japanese bonsai-style container adds
to its beauty.

An early American dry sink is used as a planter for variegated ivy, philo-dendron, and a blooming azalea. The removable metal pan can be carried outside in summer. The blooming plant is in a separate pot which can be exchanged when out of bloom for another seasonal flower. (Larry Gordon)

Foliage is washed clean by dashing rainstorms, so it is no wonder plants grown indoors need occasional washing with warm water. It helps cut the oily film and makes the wetting more thorough. A film of dust and grime on leaves may drastically cut down on the amount of light entering a leaf and may cause it to react as if it were in eternal deep shade. Under these conditions plants fail to grow normally regardless of the amount of light you give them. Lethal temperatures are quickly attained if hot sunlight inadvertently hits the leaf. This causes "sunburn"—brown spots which appear only where the leaf surface is exactly at right angles to the sun.

Plants in the jungle are never subjected to drafts of furnace-dry air. Keep your plants away from hot-air registers or radiators that create currents. Similarly, doors that open directly outside and allow drafts of sub-zero cold to enter cause tropical plants to suffer.

It is the planter mix which is the most crucial for indoor plants. To understand this, we go again to the tropics, the home of our indoor-outdoor plants. Soil in the jungle is far different from our garden soil. Vast quantities of raw organic matter accumulate in thick layers on the jungle floor. This loose layer of dead leaves and branches inter-mixed with the surface roots of plants has a very low mineral content.

Planter mixes are far superior to potting soils for tropical plants because the coarse organic matter simulates conditions in the jungle, allows sharp drainage but has high water-retaining capacity. But planter mixes have one drawback. They are difficult to wet. You must thoroughly soak the planter mix before you use it; when it is very dry it will actually repel water. The use of dry planter mix will often create problems, such as the water coursing through the mix without actually wetting it. Sometimes when plants are neglected for long periods, the planter mix will dry out. Then the only way to wet it is to soak the container in a bucket or tub of water. Usually two to three hours soaking is sufficient to thoroughly wet the planter mix. After the container is allowed to drain completely, it is returned to its usual spot.

One more word of warning: if you have a lovely container that doesn't have drainage, use it as a jardiniere. Put the plant in a clay pot inside the jardiniere with a rack two or three inches high under it. Or, after you water, pour out the water that goes through the pot into the jardiniere. Never let a pot stand in water for longer than a few hours.

192

(Robert C. Cleveland)

(Far left) Here a Kentia palm in a portable box can be moved outdoors in summer and grows inside in the cold months. It is the palm used extensively in hotel lobbies and executive suites and withstands almost any abuse without showing it.

(Left) This tall ti plant, Cordyline terminalis, *is a good example of a tropical indoor-outdoor plant that is at home in either location as long as temperatures are above forty degrees.*

Another way to grow in containers and prevent moisture from seeping through to floors and carpets is to use the technique of double potting. For this you obtain a handsome ceramic or metal jardiniere that will accept a clay pot of the largest size. Put the potted plant in the planter and fill in the space under it and between the walls with peat moss. This will absorb all of the extra water you give the plant and keep the soil in the pot moist but not wet. Fertilize once a month with fish tablets.

To get an idea of how much water to give a container, leave a glass of water on the table or floor beside it and mark the level of the water. When you water apply an amount equal to that lost in evaporation to the entire surface of the planter. Thus if the water drops a half inch in the tumbler, apply a half inch depth of water over the entire container. This will give you a rule of thumb that will be a guide as to how often to water and how much to apply.

194

Chapter XI

TROPICAL PLANTINGS

**Hardy Plants with the
Bold Look of the Tropics**

The lush tropical feeling of the gardens of Hawaii and the South Seas can be achieved even in cold climates with plants that have bold foliage resistant to winter cold. If you don't want to turn your entire garden to these plants it is easy to create a bower that goes with the trade winds and tropic skies. You will want to select a warm, quiet place with very rich, humusy soil and ample moisture.

True mainstays of the garden are plants that must die back to the ground in cold weather but quickly shoot up with the advent of spring. A good example is bear's-breech (*Acanthus mollis*). This plant has such a striking leaf that it was used by the ancient Greeks as a model for the capitals of their columns. The leaves are up to three feet long and have an incised margin. One plant alone makes a lush scene and

Tropical leaves have a variety of textures, as shown here. The refined foliage of the needle evergreen, podocarpus, often called fern pine, drips from the top of the picture. But the preponderance of foliage pattern is composed of huge, bold leaves, such as the liana in the right corner. Ferns, begonia and the mottled leaves of the gold-dust tree complete the ensemble. Most of these cannot be grown out-of-doors where winters are cold but there are bold-leaved plants, ferns, bamboos, and other tropical appearing plants that you can use anywhere to make a junglelike landscape.

TROPICAL PLANTINGS

195

A most tropical leaf is that of the fancy-leaved caladium, a tuberous-rooted perennial. The tubers must be lifted and stored where the ground freezes but they grow quickly if set out after danger of frost is past. It is an ideal decoration for a warm, shaded location and combines well with ferns and tuberous begonias to make a tropical setting.

196

One of the best of the large-leaved hardy plants is the one we call bear's-breech, but the ancient Greeks called it acanthus. Its beautiful leaves were so much admired they were used as the leaf motif on the top of their columns. This plant will survive winters below zero and will grow rapidly in the spring to form a clump of deeply lobed and cut leaves up to three feet long. From the center of this arises a three-foot flower spike set with white flowers. It thrives in a moist, shady location.

(Left) The giant leaves of the elephant's-ear attain a length of six feet—will tear in the wind if not planted in a protected location. Colocasia esculenta (its scientific name) forms its mammoth leaves from tuberous roots that must be dug and stored over winter where the soil freezes hard. It is the taro root of the tropics, a source of the food called poi in the South Seas. The leaves are damaged at thirty degrees so do not set out the tuber until all danger of frost is past. Grow in rich, wet soil. If you grow it in a planter-box you can bring it indoors in winter and the leaves will stay green. Combine it with canna, ferns, and palms in containers for a truly tropical effect.

(Below) This giant hibiscus bloom grows in any garden in the country. This is one of the Henderson hybrids known as 'Super Clown' with flowers up to twelve inches in diameter. The bush dies to the ground in winter but attains six to eight feet in rich soil and blooms until frost.

One of the most appealing of all bold-leaved hardy shrubs is the bottle-brush buckeye, Aesculus parviflora. *In spring when it is covered with foot-long panicles of white flowers it is unbelievably beautiful. The huge leaves with five to seven leaflets are decorative from spring to fall. It can be propagated by root cuttings, is hardy to below zero, takes shade or full sun.*

when the flowering stalk rises four to five feet, it will make an arresting accent. The spikes carry tubular white, rose or lilac flowers with green or purple spiny bracts. It grows best in semishade. A similar effect can be created in the sun with the annual castor-bean, but it must be planted each year in the cold areas. The palmately lobed leaves are often two feet wide and the plant may attain twelve feet in a single season.

Another plant that requires annual planting but grows from a bulb that may be stored is the colorful fancy-leaved caladium. It requires warm shade for best effect and wherever this can be provided, they may be started indoors, and taken out when all danger of frost is past and hot weather begins. The greenleafed elephant's-ear (*Colocasia esculenta*) will form its giant arrowhead-shaped leaves when planted in the spring, and after frost has killed its leaves, can be dug and stored.

The spotted *Ligularia,* called leopard plant, has large round tropical-appearing leaves. It is a shade plant and tuberous rooted but the roots survive down to zero-degrees in winter and grow again in the spring. The bold leaved *Bergenia* (sometimes called saxifrage) is in the same category.

Bamboo confers a tropical effect and there are species that are hardy in the coldest areas of the country. The hardiest bamboo is the yellow groove, *Phyllostachys aureosulcata,* which survives twenty degrees below zero. Several endure temperatures down to zero, including the giant timber *P. bambusoides* and the golden *P. aurea.* More hardy is the green bamboo, *P. viridis,* which takes temperatures to ten degrees below. All mentioned are of the running type whose roots must be confined in a tub or tile or they will spread throughout the garden. Giant reedgrass, *Arundo donax,* which resembles bamboo, is hardy in Ohio and can be grown in containers farther north.

The most tropical appearing of all shrubs is the perennial *Hibiscus,* especially the Henderson hybrids of *H. moscheutos,* which produce flowers as startling and dramatic as those of the tropical Chinese hibiscus. They attain twelve inches in diameter and the shrub grows rapidly to six or eight feet. 'Raspberry Rose,' 'New Blood Red,' 'Apple Blossom,' and 'Super Clown' are good varieties. They die to the ground in winter and bounce back the next year with another succession of beautiful flowers. Slightly less hardy is the Confederate-rose, *H. mutabilis,* with flowers opening white and changing to pink and red.

SPOT GARDENS

200

(Left) Hardly a plant for a small garden is the giant-leaved gunnera. The leaves attain eight feet on soft spined petioles up to six feet long. The leaf blade is roughly veined and the margin cut and lobed in a distinctive fashion. In cold areas leaves die back in winter but the plants survive temperatures down to zero. Grow in moist rich soil in a shaded location. Its dominant size makes it ideal as a focal point beside a large swimming pool. The plant should be used by itself and given a lot of room.

(Below) While helleborus is not a tropical plant it has a tropical appearance and can be grown in any area of the country. Combined with ferns and aralia in a shady location, the foliage makes an interesting texture. It has green flowers early in spring and they remain attractive into the summer. Plant in soil supplied with ample humus and give water in drought periods.

(Right) Candlebush is a tropical yellow-flowered bush that grows so rapidly from seed it forms a full-sized shrub in one season. The flowers are in candelabralike clusters and appear in the fall. The feathery leaves contrast with canna and other simple-leaved plants. It takes sun and drought and grows in any well-drained soil.

(Below) The leopard plant is the name of a bold-leaved perennial, hardy to zero. The common variety, 'Aureo-maculata,' has round, yellow spots or splotches on the kidney-shaped leaves. Another handsome variety, 'Argenteum,' has leaves with white borders. Farfugium (formerly called Ligularia), needs shade and makes a tropical scene combined with ferns and other large-leaved shade plants.

(Left) Any tropical garden worthy of the name should include bamboo. The pygmy type shown here can be used as a groundcover. Here it combines with juniper and rocks to make a tropical setting.

(Below) Plantain-lily (Hosta plantaginea) gives a tropical touch when used as a groundcover. The large heart-shaped leaves have a shiny surface and are deeply and distinctively veined. Grow in sun or heavy shade. The flowers of this variety are fragrant with perfume of the tropics.

(Right) Tuberous begonias have the strange and beautiful flowers we associate with the tropics. They are native to the Torrid Zone, at home in the jungles of South America. But because the tubers can be lifted and stored, we can grow them anywhere. Here the basket-type is used along with the erect form to bring the beauty and subtle fascination of the jungle to this garden.

(Below) The hardiest of all tropical fruit trees is the loquat. Its large, shiny leaves hint its origin. Here it is grown in a planter supplied with casters so it may be moved in and out depending on the temperature. Loquat will withstand down to twenty degrees above without damage but it flowers in the winter-time, and flower buds are killed by below-freezing temperatures. Flowers are white, small, and not attractive but the fruit, up to two inches in diameter is tasty.

The taller yellow-groove bamboo withstands twenty degrees below zero but it spreads by underground runners if it is not confined in a submerged tile. It will grow in any soil and needs little care or attention. Use it for a vertical accent in full sun, with broad-leaved plants to confer a tropical appearance to the garden.

Althea or rose-of-Sharon is an erect deciduous shrub growing about ten feet tall with flowers which resemble those of the tropical hibiscus. They bloom from early July to frost and are hardy to New York and Ontario, Canada.

Another dependable accent for tropical gardens in a cold climate is the banana relative, canna. Large rich green to bronzy leaves and trusses of flowers in shades of yellow, pink, and red make a show in summer. Wherever the ground freezes, the plants have to be dug and stored over winter. The Pfitzer Dwarf varieties grow only thirty inches tall and are suitable for containers. Cannas are a good choice near the pool, as their leaves do not fall but must be trimmed.

The bold foliage of the canna contrasts pleasingly with the cut leaves of dahlia, another truly tropical flower. The dwarf "annual" or bedding dahlias don't have to be staked. They come in both pompon and single types, with blooms only two inches in diameter. The huge eight- to ten-inch blooms of the giant dahlias are produced on plants at least five feet high.

In the shade, hellebores and hosta (plantain-lily) furnish tropical accents which make a great contrast with the refined foliage of ferns. There are two kinds of *Helleborus*, one that blooms in late winter, known as the Christmas-rose, and the one that blooms in spring, called the Lenten-rose. They require cool, moist shade. The foliage stays green all winter in contrast to the hosta, which dies back. Its leaves are heart-shaped and distinctly veined. Clusters of lilylike flowers appear in summer. Varieties with blue-green leaves take more sun exposure than the variegated or solid green kinds. A hardy calla-lily variety, 'Crowborough,' might succeed in cold areas but other varieties must be dug and stored like gladiolus.

Ferns whose fronds attain great size are the more tropical in appearance but these unfortunately require more room. Sometimes the ferns can be grown perched on the top of a tree trunk to simulate a tree fern of the tropics.

There is no more tropical appearing tree than the hardy catalpa, with its huge leaves and clusters of trumpet-shaped flowers. Less hardy is the similar Empress tree (*Paulownia*). The leaves may be increased to nearly two feet in diameter by annual pruning to the ground, but flower production is curtailed. The flower buds which are formed in fall are always subject to damage by cold.

Huge compound leaves are the characteristic of the weed tree

Several trees can be said to have tropical aspects but the largest leaves of any hardy tree are carried by the Chinese angelica. Pictured is a single leaf of Aralia chinensis.

You may think the fig tree is too tropical for your garden but they will grow outdoors as far North as Pittsburgh, Pennsylvania, if they are given winter protection. Usually straw or bundles of hay are wrapped around the trunk and main limbs of the plant. It is pruned severely but starts growth early and produces ripe fruits in late summer until frost. Here a fig is espaliered on a wall to give it the extra reflected heat needed for early and rapid growth.

214

All ferns display a truly tropical aspect by their luxurious growth. Any warm, quiet location where the soil is rich and moisture is ample suits these adaptable plants. Some accept full sun but most want shade. Good drainage and light porous soil are needed to keep them thriving.

called the tree-of-heaven or *Ailanthus*. Very hardy and fast-growing, it fares well under extremes of climate and soil. Another bold-leaved tree from China is the angelica (*Aralia chinensis*) with huge compound leaves up to three feet long. It is hardy to Ontario, Canada.

Several annual vines including the common morning-glory give a tropical aura with lush foliage and beautiful flowers. Cup-and-saucer vine, if started early indoors, will make a twenty-foot growth by means of its twining tendrils.

Chapter XII

ORIENTAL INFLUENCE

Easy Maintenance with Japanese Gardens

The serenity and contemplative mood conferred by a Japanese garden is not its only advantage. A very modern advantage attained is the low maintenance required. A walled American garden is screened to allow privacy in relaxation, not designed for the Japanese concept of revery and communing with nature.

Japanese gardens are well-adapted to small areas where space is at a premium as so often occurs in the city. A location shaded by high walls and lofty buildings is suitable and if the soil is sterile and rocky no matter. Here you can utilize arrangements of rocks and pebbles and select a few choice plants that will survive in such a place. The basic plantings require very little attention.

Groundcovers are used instead of grass lawns. In sunny spots, plants such as Irish-moss and sea thrift require no mowing while mondo-grass or pachysandra fill shaded areas. No annual flower beds with all their attendant hard work are tolerated. Instead, perennial flowers are used as isolated specimens set off by rocks or beds of

Restraint is of paramount importance to the Japanese garden. The oriental deplores more than incidental use of flowers as a potential disturbing influence. This wooden bridge leading to circular stepping stones across a pool is a fine example.

Short pieces of tree trunks set vertically make headers for the planting beds. An azalea in full bloom, heavenly-bamboo (left), Japanese pittosporum (left and right), juniper, and lily-turf complete the picture of serenity surveyed by the seated Buddha. Circles of sea thrift will spread to form a solid turflike groundcover.

218

A simple teahouse with a moon window is kept private by a bamboo fence.
Pines, sculptured shrubs, and bamboo are the basic landscape plants, all in
keeping with the oriental conception.

(Left) A bamboo pipe is the source of the water that flows over river-washed pebbles through lichen-covered rocks. Fern, bamboo, and pines are used in this garden.

(Below) This stone bridge leads to millstones used as stepping stones across the pond. At the right a revetment made of bamboo set vertically marks the shoreline. Lanterns reflected in the water throughout this garden designed for walking, make a delicate and understated view at night.

(Right) A wooden arching bridge, traditional in the Japanese garden is kept in scale by a weeping willow whose drooping branches touch their mirror image in the water.

(Below) This stone bridge is edged with a bundle of reeds tied together with rope. A single plant of rockspray cotoneaster is the only decoration.

Natural stone has an important place in the Japanese garden. Mountain stones such as these are used in arrangements that have symbolical or spiritual form. The vertical element signifies the guardian rock. Usually two or four others are used with it, one flat—the other rounded, which create a scene for peaceful contemplation.

225

Dry stream beds filled with river pebbles symbolize water and tufts of lily-turf are used at the shoreline and near rocky islands to make the sensation of rushing water more real.

pebbles. Iris, lilies, daylily, *Saxifraga*, plantain-lily (*Hosta*), and turf-lily (*Liriope*), are some of the plants at home in a Japanese garden. Trees most often desired are maple (especially the cut-leaved variety), ginkgo, sweet gum, pines, flowering plum, peach and cherry, and weeping willow. Star, Yulan, and common saucer magnolia as well as dogwood also fit in.

An excellent variety of shrubs belong in this garden: camellia and azalea, aucuba (gold-dust plant), barberries, flowering quince, hydrangea, junipers, holly, holly-grape, heavenly-bamboo (*Nandina*), sweet-olive, pittosporum, cotoneaster, and euonymus. Bamboo of all kinds are natural here, as well as spruce, Lawson's cypress, and wisteria.

Massive effects are obtained with carefully selected rocks, chosen for size, shape, or color. They are usually placed in small groups of odd numbers and arranged according to height, an art as difficult and intricate as a flower arrangement. The color of the rocks and their embellishment with lichens and moss is of great value to the landscape. Rocks are usually set deeply with a small part above ground, so that any sense of instability is avoided and the impression of latent strength is conveyed.

The most elegant ornament is the stone lantern which evolved in India, China, and Korea before being adopted by the Japanese. The lanterns come in a bewildering variety of shapes and sizes, legged and traditional. The ultimate in grace and beauty is the snow-viewing lantern. Other ornaments are stone fish, raccoons, and metal cranes and turtles. Statues of Buddha are also popular.

Water is the second most important element in the Japanese garden. Sometimes this is merely a bamboo pipe dripping into a stone basin, but a pond or stream adds immeasurably to the garden scene. Of course it is not always possible to have water in the garden and some ingenius ways of simulating streams, waterfalls, and ponds have been invented. By the use of vertical rocks, a waterfall is suggested, while streams and ponds are imitated by means of water-worn pebbles. The "stream" banks are marked by larger rocks with typical pond-edge plants such as rushes and sedges. Or, you can make a small replica of the famous sand garden of Ryoan-yi in Kyoto. A small rectangle of fine white sand raked to indicate ripples with classic groupings of rock create the effect of dark islands jutting from the water.

ORIENTAL INFLUENCE

(Right) Huge boulders set vertically symbolize a waterfall and the sand or gravel stream bed meanders among the rocks.

(Below) Of all the plants, the most unusual is the bulrush or horsetail (Equisetum). It is a fine vertical accent but it must be confined or it will spread by underground runners throughout the garden.

230

(Left) Traditional is the flowering cherry tree, which makes the garden lovely in spring. Flowering fruit trees are the only flamboyant element in this garden.

(Below) One of the unusual aspects of a Japanese garden is called the "borrowed scene technique," in which a nearby landscape is utilized as an integral part of the garden. Here a wide sloping lawn leads to a view of a eucalyptus grove.

(Right) A screen may be used to hide unsightly features. This woven bamboo structure is called a sodigaki.

(Below) Japanese gardens are all fenced and must have gates in keeping with the material used for the walls. While the main gate is often a tile roofed structure, this simple bamboo gate suffices for a light and airy bamboo fence.

(Left) This light and open sodigaki *lends a hint of privacy to the patio beyond. The pathway which detours around the screen gives notice of the approach of company.*

(Below) This wooden gate decorated with reed panels is used to harmonize with a reed fencing. The branches of this broomlike reed are cut off evenly at the top for a neat and even line.

FENCES AND GATES

The walls of Japanese houses are composed of sliding screens that open on all sides to the garden. This makes the garden walls virtually the exterior walls of the house. Fences are also used as partitions to separate views and sometimes are a stage on which to display or form a background for plants. Depending on its use, the fence is generally made of bamboo, closely or loosely woven. Gates are of simple construction, usually of the same material as the fence.

PATHS AND STEPS

One of the strong features is the path made of native or cut stone, though often of earth outlined with logs. Stepping stones are used to provide access to the inner reaches of the garden. In more elaborate gardens, a stone or wooden bridge leads across a stream.

238

Chapter XIII

KITCHEN GARDENS

Useful and Edible Plants
Close at Hand

The "kitchen garden" in our day has come to mean a small space adjacent to the back door where a few herbs and vegetables will grow and provide fresh things for the table. Most herbs will fit this definition but if you attempt to grow all of them your garden will easily extend beyond its bounds. Vegetables, too, must be selected carefully or the kitchen garden will be bigger than the house and just as unwieldy. The trick is to turn out an adequate garden in a limited space.

To limit the size of her herb garden, our great grandmother used a wagon wheel with the spokes delineating the space for each kind.

Every home needs fresh chives, not only through the spring and summer, but clumps dug in the fall and kept going in the kitchen window to furnish flavoring for salad, omelettes, soup, new potatoes, and dozens of gourmet dishes. Potato salad without fresh chives is a natural disaster.

The nine other herbs most often used are sage, mint, parsley, oregano, basil, sweet marjoram, thyme, rosemary, and borage. Of

Parsley is used as a groundcover in this rose bed. Its crinkly foliage is as attractive as any ornamental plant, yet a patch this size will provide all the garnish you can use.

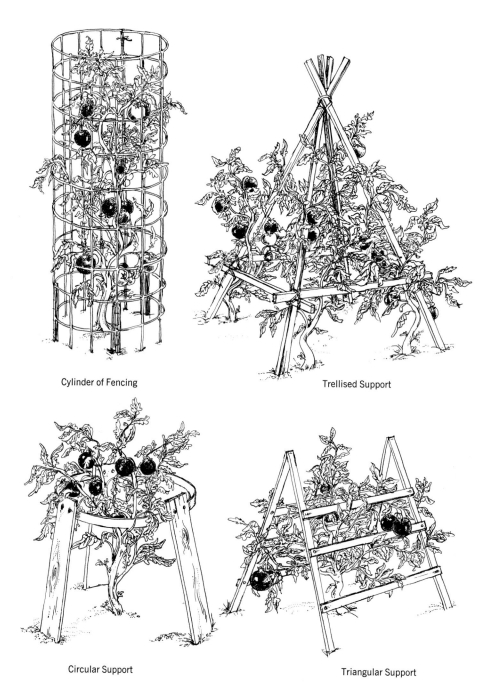

Cylinder of Fencing

Trellised Support

Circular Support

Triangular Support

Tomatoes may be trained in various ways. A single stake may hold one or two vines and one plant, if the shoots are properly pinched when the plant is small, will produce twice as much fruit as vines trained on separate stakes. A framework can support tomatoes without training. The best device of all is a cylinder of wire fencing.

240

Cherry tomatoes grow and ripen right on the windowsill. This is the 'Atom,' and there are several other kinds that vary greatly in flavor. They all do well in hanging baskets.

A

B

these, basil, borage, parsley, and sweet marjoram are annuals or treated as annuals in most areas. The remainder are planted but once. All require a sunny location as do the vegetables.

Although radishes are one of the fastest crops from seed to harvest (some varieties requiring only twenty-one days), they are not important enough to give valuable dooryard space. Unless you want some of the unusual kinds such as 'Icicle' or the summer radish called 'Strassburg,' which the Germans eat with beer, the radishes you find at the market will have as good quality and be inexpensive as the ones you can grow.

Leaf lettuce, however, is very much worth growing and in successive crops. Because you can harvest as much or as little as you need for daily use—the plants will continue to produce—a short row is enough for the average family. When the lettuce is only a few inches tall the row may be thinned and the plants used as the early crop.

Spinach is no longer exclusively a cool weather crop because new varieties such as 'Tampala' extend the season into the hot weather. Unless your summers are very cool or you can grow in the winter it is best not to try kale. However, anyone can grow Swiss chard, usually called summer greens. They may be harvested by removing the outer leaves and allowing the center to develop, or the entire plant may be cut off three inches above the crown and new leaves will be produced.

Beets and carrots are a mainstay in the kitchen garden. For an average family you need only about a ten-foot row of each. The new 'Golden' beet gives you all the flavor without the red juice, which for many is the greatest drawback for beets at the table. In salads, this beet does not have the attractive color but is quite a conversation piece. You might even trick a beet-shy youngster into eating this one. Beet "seed" is really a capsule containing four seeds, each of which may form a plant. Remember this when planting or you will have a lot more thinning to do. 'Nantes' is still the best carrot for the home garden but for heavy soils, 'Oxheart' or 'Short 'n Sweet' are the better choices.

A couple of clumps of summer squash is sufficient to provide the average family, if spaced two-by-two feet apart. Zucchini is the big favorite, but it should be picked when no more than four inches long and an inch thick. Peppers and eggplants should not be neglected. If you keep the fruits picked, they will continue to bear until frost, so don't plant too many.

With limited space you can still grow many of the vegetables such as snapbeans, cucumbers, and tomatoes. These can be trained vertically. Pole beans are the answer for the small garden and their reward is fine flavor. You will never go back to bush beans once you have tasted the 'Kentucky Wonder.' Or try the long purple French pole beans for a change. Cucumbers, too, can be grown on a trellis or wire fence.

The best way to limit the spread of tomatoes is to provide a cylinder of fencing to keep each plant erect and productive. Of course they can be staked but pinching each of the side shoots is a tedious and never-ending job. Cherry tomatoes are sometimes grown in hanging baskets to conserve space but here they are more decorative than practical.

An earthen pyramid constructed with an eight-inch-wide steel lawn edging can double the productivity of a small space. Corrugated steel is better for this purpose than the softer aluminum strips often sold. Thirty feet costs only about $9.00 and ninety feet about $25.00. You could make concentric circles or rectangles, each in a set-back from the lower level, reducing each level by three feet in diameter and make a bed that would produce all of these kitchen vegetables and herbs in an area less than ten-feet wide.

A pyramid is an ideal device for growing strawberries. Everbearing types such as 'Red Rich' are ideal for this purpose, as they bear heavily in spring and continue until frost.

USE IN LANDSCAPING

You can always have a supply of herbs, strawberries, and certain vegetables if you incorporate them into your landscape plans. For instance, one of the best groundcovers in sun or light shade is the wild strawberry whose succulence is legendary. An improved type called 'No. 25,' the result of a cross between the wild and the commercial types, is widely grown. A fair-sized lawn patch will produce all the berries you want in a season. Everbearing varieties such as 'Ozark Beauty' are vigorous enough to use this way.

Thyme, prostrate rosemary, catmint, sweet woodruff, winter

Mints are delightful to have around for refreshing drinks, for flavoring lamb and other meat, and for many other uses. Seed comes up thickly and must be transplanted. When mature, its roots should be contained to prevent it from spreading all over the garden.

Strawberries can be grown in a small space by utilizing a strawberry jar. The jar is filled with an acid planter mix—one containing peat moss. The center usually has a pottery or hardware cloth cylinder to allow water to penetrate to the bottom of the jar. Otherwise water applied to the top will flow out of the highest opening and not water the plants at the bottom.

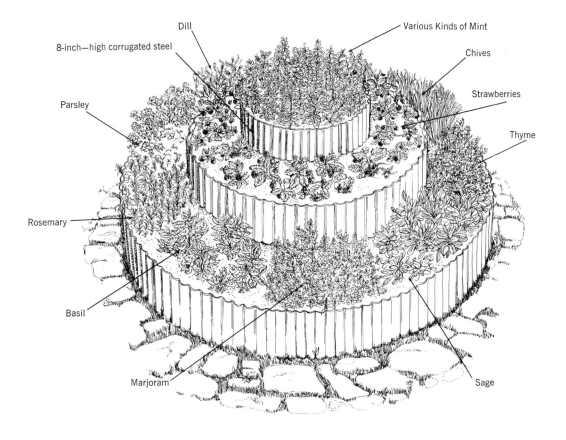

Dill

8-inch—high corrugated steel

Various Kinds of Mint

Chives

Parsley

Strawberries

Thyme

Rosemary

Basil

Marjoram

Sage

The Pyramid Garden—it can be circular or rectangular.

247

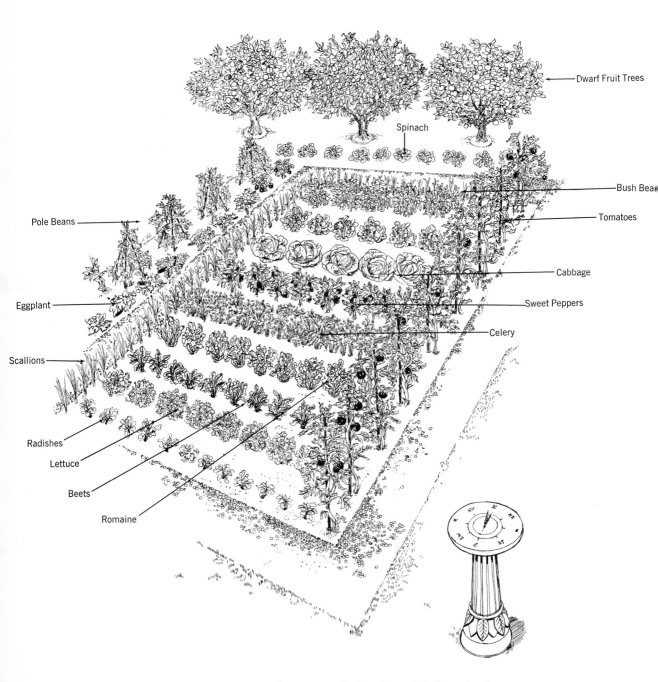

Dwarf Fruit Trees

Spinach

Bush Beans

Tomatoes

Pole Beans

Cabbage

Sweet Peppers

Eggplant

Celery

Scallions

Radishes

Lettuce

Beets

Romaine

A suggested plan for a Kitchen Garden.

248

savory, and camomile are some of the herbs that double as ground-covers. Jewel mint, while not of culinary importance, is wonderfully fragrant planting for use between stepping stones.

Parsley and basil (especially the variety 'Dark Opal') are striking enough to grace any border, and a bed of blue curled Scotch kale is a double delight. Swiss chard, asparagus, and rhubarb have beautiful enough leaves to be grown as ornamentals. In areas to which it is adapted, the artichoke is a stunning garden accent.

Chapter XIV

The Crowning Touch

There is no better way to transform a niche than with a bit of statuary or other work of art. Birdbaths and sundials are out of fashion but bas-relief sculpture, mosaics, and statues are becoming quite popular. Natural sculptures composed of rocks or driftwood also give a rustic touch in the garden. The gardener can also find a wide variety of copies of ancient art reproduced in fiber glass. Replicas of the Aztec sun calendar, Grecian plaques, Siamese heads, pre-Columbian figures, and Egyptian and Persian fragments may, in just the right place, become wall decorations.

MOSAICS AND MURALS

Perhaps the most exciting art is the expressive use of tile, pebbles, or shells in creating an original design. With these or selected pieces of driftwood you can make a garden unique with relatively little effort.

Simple designs can be ingenious and beautiful. Here posts carved in an interesting fashion are studded with nails to make an original sculpture unique.

ART

251

The three garden graces—Aglaia (Brilliance), Euphrosyne (Joy), and Thalia (Bloom)—in this bas-relief make a fine ornament that can be obtained at a surprisingly low cost.

This shrine to St. Anthony brings a meditative spirit to the garden.

A fiber-glass replica of a pre-Columbian sculpture is displayed on a garden wall.

A porcelain vase, too large for the average home, becomes a handsome decoration in the garden that is an important enlivening factor in this rather ordinary corner.

256 *St. Francis stands amid the strawberry groundcover and Palos Verde rock, diminished by the giant yucca.*

An ages-old plaque with Japanese characters—a shrine to the god   257
Bodhisattva—sits on the ground in peaceful contemplation.

258

This dramatic bronze figure is called "Ahab" by sculptor Ray Jensen of Bellevue, Washington.

The ultimate in garden art is the mural or wall painting, often seen in Europe and Mexico but an art form which has languished in the United States. Bold colors brighten up walls which would otherwise be dark and forbidding. Usually earthy colors should be chosen since they compose well with green vegetation.

If you feel that your artistic ability is not up to such a creative effort, you might find much greater latitude in mosaic; the lovely patterns made with tile, bits of glass, or pebbles can make rich, interesting ornamentation. For the beginner, ceramic tiles are easiest to work with, as they require little cutting and are easily adapted to a geometric design. After the design and color are worked out on paper the same size as the finished work, the lines of the design can be transferred to a waterproof (outdoor) plywood base. Tiles can be glued to plywood and spaced one-sixteenth to one-eighth inch apart to allow room for the grout—made of plaster and cement. This mixture is diluted with water to the consistency of thick cream and worked into spaces between tile with a dampened sponge. The grout should not be allowed to dry rapidly, so the process usually takes at least an hour to set. Cover the finished product with damp cloths to retard drying. Any film of grout that adheres to the tile can be removed later with a damp cloth. After two or three days, when the mosaic is completely dry, it should be given a coat of plastic resin to make it waterproof.

Ceramic tiles give a smooth and even surface, but Venetian glass mosaic has a rough texture that gives an extra sparkle to the design. It is much more effective, as the tiles can be cut with a tile snipper to any desired shape and may be arranged edgewise with greater leeway. Designs with curved lines are also more easily accomplished with glass tiles. Another glass tile, called tessara, has the most brilliant colors. This same kind of tile appeared in the famous mosaics of Byzantium.

Pebbles from a fast stream, shells from the ocean, pieces of water-worn driftwood, and other interesting objects picked up on the beach are a natural medium for the garden. But heavy pebbles are of course better suited for paving than for walls.

One of the best places to find driftwood is near a large body of water. After the ice has melted in the spring the windward side of a lake will be strewn with driftwood. But driftwood need not be only those gnarled and twisted pieces of wood that have been cast up on the shore. You can discover good specimens in orchards, woodlots, ART

259

260

(Left) A wooden figure of a bighorn mountain goat with owls sitting on its knees is the work of Dudley C. Carter of Bellevue, Washington. It is carved in black walnut.

(Below) The bronze dog baying to the moon is entitled "Misty" by its creator, G. Alan Wright of Renton, Washington.

(Left) *This formal sculpture garden with a Grecian figure carrying an urn is complemented by the Italian cypress and the twisted juniper (in the planter). Cinerarias make the area come alive with their colors.*

(Below) *The lighted sculpture is enhanced by a simple fountain to make a dramatic night view that would otherwise be black and dismal.*

264

(Left) This fountain made of stone is a carp, revered by the Japanese as a symbol of success overcoming adversity. The carp, like our salmon, swims upstream against terrific odds to spawn.

(Below) Art forms need not be expensive. This piece of bleached driftwood with the bleached bones creates a mood in a small space.

This modern sculpture of metal, created with a welding torch, is the cynosure of all eyes.

roadsides, pastures, deserts, and deep in the forest or high in the mountains. Many tree branches can be made into driftwood.

Roots and stumps often make desirable objects but when they have been gouged out by heavy ice floes they are heavily water-soaked and dark in color. It may take practice to see their hidden beauty but after a period of drying and sandblasting the color and grain of the twisted roots and branches will be revealed. Although sandblasting is the easiest way to clean driftwood it may be done with steel wool or with a wire brush. If it already has the desired silver patina it need only be washed using a soft brush. The sunbleached finish can be restored by a week or two in the hot sun, wetting it occasionally. Rubbing chalk in blemishes with the fingers effectively disguises them. Before cleaning cut away unwanted parts, keeping in mind the effect you wish to create. Such pieces can be used effectively in your garden to create dramatic accents, and prove that art need not be expensive.

Sculpture in the garden actually originated in pagan Greece and Italy, and was revived when ancient figures were unearthed in excavations. Their use spread throughout France and Italy with the development of formal gardens. Since the English climate was unsuited to marble, where freezing would damage it, lead became the medium for a wealth of designs created especially for gardens.

As sculpture replicas range from the miniature to the gargantuan, cost may vary from negligible to quite expensive. Selection of the right size is important because of the scale of the surroundings. The same object can be equally unsatisfactory if it is too large or too small. Plants should always be chosen to compliment the art work, never to compete with it. Great care must be utilized in the selection of such art pieces. Statues that are too formal will strike a jarring note in the natural garden but rough-hewn sculpture, bronze, or lead pieces may be appropriate. It is more difficult to place statuary in the contemporary garden but the wide array of art objects—from primitive to non-objective—will enable you to select something that achieves the desired effect. Mere suitability is not enough. The commonplace is always to be avoided. Even a fine piece such as a fawn or Pan will very soon become trite.

However, there are those garden shrines where the Marian motif remains suitable for some personalities. And, although a statue of St. Francis would seem to be the natural choice for such a sanctuary, it is St. Fiacre, the renowned hermit of Kilfera, whom gardeners invoke as their patron saint.

INDEX

Note: Page numbers in italics indicate illustrations. Throughout the index, common names for plants are followed by the Latin name in parentheses.

Abelia, 7
Acacia, *123*
Acanthus mollis, 91, 195, *197*
Aeonium, 165
Aesculus parviflora, 101, 200
Agathis robusta, 183
Agave, *147, 152*
  A. attenuata, 11, 165
Aglaonema, *108, 169*
Ailanthus altissima, 215
Ajuga, 13, *14,* 33, *53,* 57, *58, 94, 155, 162*
  bronze, 78
  purple, 89
Akebia, 30, 39
Albizia julibrissin, 123
Allegheny vine (*Adlumia*), 28
Aloe, 165
Alpine garden, 139, *140, 141, 144, 145, 146,* 157, *162*
Althea, 200–211
Alum root (*Heuchera*), 13
Ampelopsis, 39
Anacharis, 70
Andromeda, 7
Angelica tree, Chinese (*Aralia chinensis*), 212, 215
Anthurium, *113*
Aphelandra, *108*

Apple, crab (*Malus*), 43
Aralia, 4, 7, 17, *106,* 170, *203*
Aralia chinensis, 212, 215
  Japanese (*Fatsia japonica*), 6
  snowflake (*Trevesia palmata*), 183, *184*
Araliaceae, 178, 183
Araucaria excelsa, 183
Arbor, 32, 39
Arborvitae, 70
Arbutus, trailing, 13, 58
Ardisia, 7
Artemisia, Silver-king, 131
  Silvermound, *126, 162*
Artichoke, 249
Artwork in the garden, *119,* 227, *251,* 251–267
Arum-root, 58
Arundo donax, 200
Ash, *123*
Asparagus, 249
  Sprenger's, 13
Aspen, 143
Atrium, *108, 115, 175*
Aubrieta deltoidea, 146
Aucuba, 7, 227
Azalea, 3, 6, 12, 63, 75, *190, 218,* 227
Azolla, 70

Baby's-breath (*Gypsophila*), creeping, 89
Baby's-tears (*Helxine*), *113*
Bachelor's-button (*Centaurea*), 131
Bamboo, 5, 170, 183, *195*, 200, *219*, *221*, 227
  golden (*Phyllostachys aurea*), 200
  green (*Phyllostachys viridis*), 200
  heavenly (*Nandina domestica*), *159*, 170, *218*, 227
  pygmy, *207*
  yellow-groove (*Phyllostachys aureosulcata*), 5, 200, *211*
Banana-shrub (*Michelia fuscata*), 7
Banana tree (*Musa*), 69
Banyan, weeping (*Ficus benjamina*), 178
Barberry (*Berberis*), 7, 33, 143, 227
Barrenwort (*Epimedium*), 13, *34*, 58
Basil (*Ocimum*), 239, 243, 249
  Dark Opal, *162*, 249
Basket, hanging, *177*, *187*, *241*
Basket-of-gold, 162
Bayberry (*Myrica pensylvanica*), 135
Beachgrass, 135
Bean, French pole, 244
Bean, pole, 244
Bearberry (*Arctostaphylos uva-ursi*), *34*, 127, 135
Bear's-breech (*Acanthus mollis*), *91*, *195*, *197*
Bed, raised, 57, 60, 103, 111, 152
Beefwood (*Casuarina*), 123
Beet, 243
  Golden, 243
Begonia, *4*, *19*, 195
  rex, 72, *120*
  tuberous, *196*, 208
  wax, *54*
Bellflower, Serbian (*Campanula poscharskyana*), 127
Bench, 57, 58–63
Bergenia, 54, 58, *91*, *100*, 200
Bignonia, 13
Billbergia, *9*
Birch tree (*Betula*), 60
Birdbath, 65
Bird-of-paradise (*Strelitzia*), 170
  giant, 70
Bittersweet (*Celastrus*), *14*, *26*
Bleeding-heart (*Dicentra*), 58
Bloodroot (*Sanguinaria*), 58
Bluebell, Carpathian (*Campanula carpatica*), 13, 58, *142*
  Serbian (*Mertensia sibirica*), 13, 33
Blueberry (*Vaccinium*), wild, 135
Bluegrass, rough-stalked (*Poa trivialis*), 58
  shade, 58

Bonsai, *10*
Borage (*Borago officinalis*), 239, 243
Border, narrow, *91*, 99–101
Bottlebrush (*Melaleuca*), *129*, 135
Bougainvillea, 30, 170
Brassaia, 178, 183
Bromeliad, *113*, *120*, 170
Broom, 135
  Scotch, *129*
Brunfelsia, 7, *12*
Buckeye, bottlebrush (*Aesculus parviflora*), *101*, 200
Buckthorn, *43*, *129*, 135
Bugleweed (*Ajuga*), 13
Bulrush (*Equisetum*), 228
Bunchberry (*Cornus canadensis*), 13, *51*, 58
Burro-tail (*Sedum morganianum*), 187

Cabomba, 70
Cactus, barrel, *147*, *151*, *152*
  Chollo, *152*
  columnar, *151*
  prickly-pear, *151*, *152*
  Saguaro, *152*
Caladium, 58, *105*, *196*, 200
Calceolaria, 3
Calla-lily 'Crowborough' (*Zantedeschia*), *211*
Calliandra, *43*
Camellia, 7, *63*, *101*, 227
  'Mystery,' 170
Camomile (*Anthemis nobilis*), 249
Campanula, *126*, *142*
Canary-bird-vine (*Tropaeolum peregrinum*), 27
Candlebush (*Cassia alata*), 204
Candytuft, perennial (*Iberis sempervirens*), 162
Canna, *11*, *199*, 204, *211*
  Pfitzer Dwarf, *211*
Caragana, 33, *123*
Carrot, 243
Castor-bean (*Ricinus communis*), 200
Casuarina, 131
Catalpa, 211
Catmint (*Nepeta cataria*), 244
Cat's-claw (*Doxantha unguis-cati*), 30
Cattail, miniature (*Typha minima*), 70
Cedar (*Cedrus*), *130*
  Atlas (*Cedrus atlantica*), *121*
Celosia, 131
Cereus peruvianus, *151*
  p. 'Monstrosus,' *151*
Chamaedorea, 187
  elegans bella, 22
Cherry, flowering (*Prunus*), 227, 231

Chives (*Allium schoenoprasum*), 239
Christmas-rose (*Helleborus*), 211
Christmas tree, New Zealand (*Metrosideros tomentosa*), 123
Chrysanthemum, 3, 7, 65, 68, *126*
  annual, 131
Cineraria (*Senecio cruentus*), 3, 55, 263
Cinnamon-vine (*Dioscorea batatas*), 39
Cinquefoil, shrubby (*Potentilla fruticosa*), 135
Citrus, 48
  dwarf, 170
Clematis, 6, 13, 27, 28, 39
Clivia, *19*
Clockvine (*Thunbergia*), 28, 39
Cobaea, 39
Coleus, 58
Colocasia esculenta, 199, 200
Columbine (*Aquilegia*), 58
Columnea, *108*
Conifers, 183
Containers, 17, *19*, 31, 55, 103, *105*, 152, 165–193, *208*, 246
Coprosma, 135
Coral-bells (*Heuchera*), 13, 58
Coral vine (*Antigonon leptopus*), 27
Cordyline, 187
  stricta, 105
  terminalis, 105, 187, *193*
Coreopsis, 37, 54, *126*, 131, 135
  perennial, *162*
Corn plant (*Dracaena fragrans*), *105*
Cosmos, 131
Cotoneaster, 7, *34*, *43*, 127, 135, *159*, 227
  rock, 30
  rockspray, 222
Cottonwood tree (*Populus*), 51
Crassula argentea, 178
Crown-vetch, gold (*Coronilla varia*), *162*
Cryptanthus, *113*
Cucumber, 244
Cup-and-saucer (*Cobaea scandens*), 13, 28, 215
Cussonia, 183
  spicata, 183
Cycad, *113*
Cycas revoluta, 113, 173
Cyclamen, 3
Cyperus alternifolius, 165
Cypress, Italian (*Cupressus sempervirens*), 263
  Lawson's (*Chamaecyparis lawsoniana*), 227
  Monterey (*Cupressus macrocarpa*), 123, *130*

Cypress vine (*Quamoclit pennata*), 27, 28

Daffodil (*Narcissus*), 3
Dahlia, 211
Daisy, Shasta (*Chrysanthemum maximum*), *126*
Daphne, 4, 7, *12*
Daylily (*Hemerocallis*), *11*, 58, 70, 99, *126*, 135, 227
Dead nettle (*Lamium galeobdolon*), 13, 58
  golden (*Lamium galeobdolon*), *162*
Deck, 68, 71, 77, *120*, 187
Desert garden, 139, 143, *147*, *150*, *151*, *152*, 157, *162*
Dichondra, 88, 89
Dieffenbachia, *105*, *108*, *169*, 170
Dion circinalis, 113
  edule, 113
Dogwood (*Cornus*), 227
Dracaena, 69–70, *105*, *108*, *166*, 183, 187
  fragrans, 105
  indivisa, 187
Driftwood, 259–267
Duckweed (*Lemna*), 70
Dusty miller (*Centaurea*), 9, *127*, 131, *152*, *161*, *162*
Dutchman's-pipe (*Aristolochia*), 30, 39, 42

Echeveria, 36, *147*, *148*, *152*, *177*
Echium, Pride of Madeira, *126*
  Tower-of-jewels, *134*
Eggplant (*Solanum melongena esculentum*), 243
Elephant plant (*Portulacaria afra*), *165*
Elephant's-ear (*Colocasia esculenta*), 70, *199*, 200
Elm (*Ulmus*), 123
Empress tree (*Paulownia*), 211
Enkianthus, 7
Entrance, 3–24
Epimedium, 54
Equisetum, 228
Erosion, 133
Escallonia, *129*
Espalier, 9, 25, 42, *43*, 44, 45, 46, 47, 48, 99, *155*, 213
Eucalyptus, 51, *123*, 131, *231*
Euonymus, *129*, 227
  winged-bark, *43*
Evergreen, needle, 183
Everlastings, 131

Fatshedera, 6
Fence, 33–39, 68, *101*, *132*, *134*, *137*

Fence, baffled, 131
  Japanese garden, 232, 235, 236
Fern, 4, 13, *53*, 58, *59*, 70, 72, 77,
    106, 119, 195, 196, 199, 203,
    204, 211, 215, *221*
Fern, maidenhair (*Adiantum*), *113*
  rabbit's-foot (*Davallia*), 187
  staghorn (*Platycerium*), *111*
  tree (*Cibotium*), 70, 211
Fertilizer, slow-release, 187
Fescue, blue (*Festuca ovina glauca*),
    4, 78, 88, 89, 135, *139,* 152, 162
Feverfew, 'Gold Feather' (*Chrysan-
    themum parthenium*), 162
Ficus benjamina, 178
  'Decora,' 178
  elastica, 178
  e. doescheri, 178
  lyrata, 178
  retusa, 178
  r. nitida, 178
Fig (*Ficus*), 48, *213*
  creeping (*Ficus pumila*), 28, 30
  fiddle-leaved (*Ficus lyrata*), *19,*
    178
Fir (*Abies*), *130*
Firethorn, 'Tom Thumb' dwarf
    (*Pyracantha*), *14*
Fish, for the pool, 81
Flame vine (*Pyrostegia venusta*),
    28, 30
Flax, New Zealand (*Phormium
    tenax*), *106*
Fleabane (*Erigeron*), 162
Floor, flagstone, 89, *96, 97, 99*
  garden, *83–102*
Foamflower (*Tiarella cordifolia*),
    13, 58
Forsythia, weeping, 33
Fothergilla, 7
Fountain, 65, 69, 72, *221, 263, 265,*
    266
Foxglove (*Digitalis*), 58
Fuchsia, *63,* 170

Gaillardia, *124,* 131
Galax, 13, 58
Garage, *14, 19*
Gardenia, 170
Gate, Japanese garden, 232, 235, 236
Gazania, 37, *159,* 162
Gazebo, 111
Geranium, *126, 181,* 187
  fancy-leaved, *155*
  ivy, *127,* 135, 162
Germander (*Teucrium*), 152
Ghost tree (*Hedera canariensis varie-
    gata*), 178
Ginger (*Zingiber*), *51*
  wild (*Asarum*), 13, 58

Ginkgo, 227
Globeflower (*Trollius*), 58
Gold-dust plant (*Aucuba*), *101,* 227
Gold-dust tree (*Aucuba*), *195*
Golden star (*Bloomeria crocea*), 13,
    58
Grape, evergreen (*Coccoloba uvi-
    fera*), 13
Grape-ivy (*Cissus*), 13
Grape-vine (*Vitis*), 30, 42
Griselinia, 135
Groundcover, 5, 13, *14,* 37, *52,* 58,
    99, 127, 152, 162, *207, 239, 249*
Gum, sweet (*Liquidambar styraci-
    flua*), 227
Gunnera, giant-leaved, *203*

Hawthorn (*Crataegus*), 123
  English (*Crataegus oxyacantha*),
    131
  India (*Raphiolepis indica*), *129,*
    135
Heath (*Erica*), 135
Heather (*Calluna*), *129,* 135
Hebe, *129,* 135
Hedera, 178
  canariensis variegata, 178
Helichrysum petiolatum, 131–135
Hellebore, Corsican, 13
Helleborus, *54,* 58, *203,* 211
Herb, 239–243
  decorative, 244–249
Hibiscus, 170, *199,* 200
  'Apple Blossom,' 200
  Chinese (*Hibiscus rosa-sinensis*),
    200
  Confederate-rose (*Hibiscus muta-
    bilis*), 200
  moscheutos, 200
  mutabilis, 200
  'New Blood Red,' 200
  'Raspberry Rose,' 200
  'Super Clown,' *199,* 200
Hills-of-snow (*Hydrangea*), 7
Holly (*Ilex*), 7, 43, 227
  Chinese (*Ilex cornuta*), *14*
Holly-grape (*Mahonia lomariifolia;
    M. bealei*), 4, 7, 170, 227
Honeysuckle (*Lonicera*), 6, 12, 13,
    30, 39, 42
Hop, Japanese (*Humulus scandens*),
    39
Hopbush, *123*
Horsetail (*Equisetum*), 70, 228
Hosta, 13, 58, 211
  plantaginea, 207, 227
Houseleek, hen-and-chickens (*Sem-
    pervivum*), 148
House plant, washing, 190
  watering, 190, 193
Humidity, indoors, 175

Hyacinth, 3, 97
Hydrangea, 65, 227
  climbing, 13, 26, 30
  oak-leaved, 7
Hypericum, 135

Iceplant (*Cryophytum crystallinum*), 127, *159*, *161*, 162
Illumination, decorative, 19, 20, *21*, 221
Impatiens, 63
Indian-laurel (*Ficus retusa*), 178
Indoor garden, 103–121, 175, 178
Iris, 99, 135, 227
  African, *41*
  crested, 58
  Japanese, *41*, 70
Irish-moss (*Sagina*), 5, 88, 89, 217
Ivy (*Hedera*), 6, 13, 28, 30, 39, 46, 52, 58, 70, 178, 187
  Algerian (*Hedera canariensis variegata*), 52, 178
  Boston (*Parthenocissus tricuspidata*), 6, 13, 26, 30
  English (*Hedera helix*), 6, 28, 30, *31*
  variegated, *14*, 190

Jade plant (*Crassula argentea*), 178
  tree (*Crassula argentea*), 170
Japanese gardens, 217–238
Jardiniere, 190, 193
Jasmine, (*Jasminum*), 13, 42
  Confederate (*Trachelospermum jasminoides*), 25
  night-blooming (*Jasminum dichotomum*), 7
  primrose (*Jasminum mesnyi*), 33, *43*
  star (*Trachelospermum jasminoides*), 7, 13, 30, *171*
  twining (*Jasminum*), 39
Jessamine, Carolina yellow (*Gelsemium sempervirens*), 13, 27, 39
Juniper (*Juniperus*), 4, 33, 34, 39, 68, 70, 135, *139*, 143, *151*, 170, 207, *218*, 227
  columnar, 70
  Hollywood twisted, *12*
  prostrate, 152
  shore, *121*, *130*
  twisted, *263*

Kalanchoe beharensis, *172*
Kale, 243
  Blue curled Scotch, 249
Kangaroo vine (*Cissus antarctica*), *181*
Kenilworth-ivy (*Cymbalaria muralis*), 39, 53
Kitchen garden, 239–249

Koreangrass (*Zoysia japonica*), 127
Kudzu (*Pueraria lobata*), 39

Lamb's-ear (*Stachys*), 131
Lamium galeobdolon, 162
Lamppost, *14*
Lantana, 33, *34*, 127, 143–152, 162
Lavender (*Lavandula*), *12*, 126, 131
Lavender-cotton (*Santolina*), *14*, 162
Leadwort (*Ceratostigma*), 13
  blue, 25
Lenten-rose (*Helleborus*), 211
Leopard plant (*Ligularia aureomaculata*), 13, 200, 204
  'Argenteum,' 204
  farfugium, 204
Leopard's-bane, 58
Leucophyllum, 152
Leucothoe, 63
Liana, *195*
Ligularia aureo-maculata, 200, 204
Lilac (*Syringa*), 12
Lily (*Lilium*), 7, 227
Lily-of-the-valley (*Convallaria*), 13, 58
Lily-turf (*Liriope*), 13, 58, *81*, 99, 126, 135, *218*, 226
Liriope, *81*, 227
Lobelia, 58
Locust, honey (*Gleditsia*), 123
Loquat (*Eriobotrya*), 208
Lotus (*Nelumbo*), 70
Lungwort (*Pulmonaria*), 13
Lupine (*Lupinus*), 131

Madeira vine (*Boussingaultia gracilis*), 28
Magnolia, common saucer, 227
  southern, 70, 123
  star, 227
  Yulan, 227
Mahonia, 4, 7
  bealei, 170
  lomariifolia, 170
Maianthemum, *51*
Manzanita, *113*
Maple (*Acer*), 51, 227
  Japanese cut-leaved, *183*
Maranta, 108
Marigold (*Tagetes*), 3, 131
Mayflower (*Epigaea*), 58
Mazus, 13, 58
Meadow-rue (*Thalictrum*), 58
Meadowsweet (*Filipendula*), 58
Melaleuca, 135
Mint (*Mentha*), 239, 245
  jewel, 249
Mirror plant (*Coprosma*), 135
Mock-orange (*Philadelphus*), 12

Mondo-grass (*Ophiopogon japonicus*), 5, 13, *53, 81, 121,* 127, 165, 217
Moneywort, *53*
Monstera, *113, 119*
Morning-glory (*Ipomoea*), 13, 30, 215
bush, 135
ground, 25
Mosaic, 259
"Mother of Thousands" (*Saxifraga stolonifera*), 53, 97
Mound, *159–162*
Mountain-laurel (*Kalmia*), 7
Mulch, *10,* 92, 94, 135
Mural, 259
Myoporum, *123,* 135
Myriophyllum, 70
Myrtle, creeping (*Vinca*), 13
trailing (*Vinca*), 58

Nandina, 170, 227
Nasturtium (*Tropaeolum*), 131
Natal-plum (*Carissa*), 34, *127,* 135
Neanthe bella (*Chamaedorea*), 22
Neopanax, 183

Oak (*Quercus*), *123*
cork, *63*
holly, 131
Oconee-bell (*Shortia*), 13, 58
Ocotillo, *151, 152,* 165
Oleander (*Nerium*), *129,* 135, 152
Olive (*Olea*), *123*
Russian (*Elaeagnus angustifolius*), *43, 123, 131, 143*
Ophiopogon japonicus, 165
Orchid, *113,* 170
Epidendrum, *137*
Miltonia, *169*
Oregano, 239
Oreopanax, 183
peltatus, 183
Osmanthus, 4, 7, *63*

Pachysandra, 13, 58, 217
Palm, 69, *119,* 152, 183, *199*
fishtail, *103*
kentia, 22, 183, *193*
lady (*Rhapis*), 22, 183, *187, 189*
paradise, 183
parlor (*Chamaedorea*), 183, *187*
rhapis, 72, 187
sago (*Cycas revoluta*), *113, 173*
standard, 22
Papaya, wild (*Oreopanax peltatus*), 183
Papyrus, Egyptian (*Cyperus papyrus*), 70, 165
Parrot's-feather (*Myriophyllum proserpinacoides*), 70–81

Parsley (*Petroselinum*), 239, 243, 249
Partridge-berry (*Mitchella*), *51,* 58
Passion-vine (*Passiflora*), 39
Path, garden, *84, 85, 97, 99, 115*
Japanese garden, *235, 236*
Patio, 111, *113, 115, 117, 119, 121, 166, 183,* 187
Paulownia, 211
Pea tree (*Caragana*), *123*
Peach (*Prunus persica*), 48
flowering, 227
Pepper (*Capsicum*), 243
Pepperbush, sweet (*Clethra alnifolia*), 7
Pepper-cress (*Lepidium*), 243
Periwinkle (*Vinca*), 13, 25, *127,* 187
Madagascar (*Vinca*), 99
Petunia, 3, *41,* 99, 131, *151*
Philodendron, *106, 108, 113, 181, 190*
tree, 170
Phlox, 58, 162
moss, 89
Phyllostachys aurea, 200
aureosulcata, 200
bambusoides, 200
viridis, 200
Pieris, 4
Pigeon's-beak, 135
Pine (*Pinus*), *10, 75, 77, 80, 130, 139, 143,* 162, *184, 219, 221,* 227
black, 78
Dammar (*Agathis robusta*), 183
dwarf Mugho, *187*
fern (*Podocarpus*), *195*
Japanese black, 131, *184*
Mugho, 135, *187*
Norfolk Island (*Araucaria excelsa*), 183
Scotch, 131
star (*Araucaria excelsa*), *130,* 183
yew (*Podocarpus*), 170, *188*
Pinks (*Dianthus*), *5, 88, 89,* 127
Pittosporum, *129,* 135, 227
Japanese, *218*
Plantain-lily (*Hosta plantaginea*), 13, 54, 207, 211, 227
Planter mix, 190
Plum (*Prunus domestica*), 48
beach, 135
flowering, 227
Plumbago, 135
Cape, 33
Poa trivialis, 58
Podocarpus, *155, 188, 195*
Polyscias, 183
Pond, lily, 70–81
Pool, decorative, *61, 65–81, 108, 157,* 217, 221, 222, 227
swimming, 69–70, 78, 79

Poppy (*Papaver*), 131
Portable garden, *121*, 165–193
Portulacaria afra, 165
Primrose (*Primula*), 13, 58
    creeper, 81
    polyantha, *101*
Privet (*Ligustrum*), 135, 152
Pseudopanax, 183
Purple heart (*Setcreasea purpurea*), 71
Pyracantha, *14*, 45, 78, 135
Pyramid garden, 244, 247

Quince, flowering (*Chaenomeles*), 43, 99, 227

Radish, 'Icicle,' 243
    'Strassburg,' 243
Ramblers, 39
Ramonda myconi, 140
Red-cedar (*Juniperus virginiana*), 123
Reedgrass, giant (*Arundo donax*), 200
Rhododendron, 4, 7, 12
Rhubarb, 249
Rock, artificial, 74, 77, *139*, 152–157
Rock-cress (*Arabis*), 13, 33, 58, 135, 162
Rock garden, *139*–157, 162
Rock-rose (*Cistus*), 43, *129*, 135
Rose (*Rosa*), 9, 30, 33, *132*, 135
    'Blaze,' 39
    climbing, 39
    'Crimson Rambler,' 39
    'Dorothy Perkins,' 39
    floribunda, 99
    hybrid tea, 37
    'New Dawn,' 39
    rugosa, 132
Rosemary (*Rosmarinus*), 99, 135, 152, *161*, 239
    prostrate, *14*, 30–33, *34*, *127*, 152, 244
Rose-moss (*Portulaca*), *124*, 131, 152
Rose-of-Sharon (*Althaea*), 135, 200–211
Rubber, India (*Ficus elastica*), 178
Rush, 227
Rush, scouring (*Equisetum*), 70
Ryegrass (*Lolium*), 135

Sage (*Salvia*), 239
Sagittaria, miniature, 70
St. Augustinegrass (*Stenotaphrum secundatum*), 58
St. John's-wort (*Hypericum*), 162
Saltbush (*Atriplex*), 135
Salt tree (*Tamarix aphylla*), 135
Sand dune, 131

Sansevieria, *181*
Santolina, *14*, 131, 152, *161*
Sarcococca, 7, *12*
Sassafras, *123*
Savory, winter (*Satureja montana*), 244–249
Saxifraga stolonifera, 97, 227
Saxifrage (*Bergenia*), 13, *91*, *100*, 200
Schefflera (*Brassaia*), 178, *181*, 183
Schefflera actinophylla, 178
    delavayi, 183
    digitata, 183
Scotch-moss (*Sagina*), 89, 162
Screen, decorative, 17, 39–48, 67, 77, *105*, 232, 235
Sculpture, 258, 261, 263, 267
Sea-buckthorn (*Hippophae*), 135
Sea-grape (*Coccoloba uvifera*), 123, *129*
Sea-holly (*Eryngium maritimum*), 135
Seashore planting, *123*–137
Sedge (*Cyperus*), 227
Sedum, 33, 127, 152, 162, 165
    dasyphyllum, 90
    guatemalense, 177
    hardy (*Sedum rupestre*), 36
    morganianum, 177
    rupestre, 36
    spectabile, 99
    velvet (*Sedum dasyphyllum*), 90
Sempervivum, *11*, 33, 36, 99, *127*, *148*, 152, 162
Shadbush (*Amelanchier*), 135
Shade, 58, 211
Shade tree garden, *51*–63
Shooting star (*Dodecatheon*), 58
Shrub, blooming, 7, *12*
    fragrant, 7
Sidewalk, *91*, *101*
Silk tree (*Albizia julibrissin*), 123
Silver lace vine (*Polygonum aubertii*), 27, 39
Skimmia, 7
Skylight, 103, *108*, *111*, 175
Snapbean, 244
Snapdragon (*Antirrhinum*), *124*, 131
Snowberry (*Symphoricarpos albus*), 63, *129*
Snow-in-summer (*Cerastium tomentosum*), 89, 135, 162
Spanish-moss (*Tillandsia*), *113*
Spathiphyllum 'Mauna Loa,' *108*
Spinach, 243
Spruce (*Picea*), *10*, 70, 123, *130*, *139*, 162, 227
Spurge, Japanese (*Pachysandra terminalis*), 13
Squash, summer, 243
Statice, *126*, 131

Stephanandra, 7, *63*

Steps, Japanese garden, *217*, *221*, 236

Stock (*Mathiola*), *124*

Stone, in Japanese garden, *225*, *226*, *227*, *228*

Stone-cress (*Aubrieta deltoidea*), 89, *146*

Strawberry (*Fragaria*), *127*, *162*, 246
  barren (*Waldsteinia fragarioides*), 58
  beach, *127*
  groundcover, 256
  'Ozark Beauty,' 244
  'Red Rich,' 244
  wild (*Fragaria virginiana*), 244

Strawberry-begonia (*Saxifraga stolonifera*), 170

Strawberry-geranium (*Saxifraga stolonifera*), 13

Strawberry jar, 246

Succulent, *11*, *36*, *60*, *61*, 99, *139*, 147, *148*, *149*, 162, *172*, *174*, *177*

Sumac (*Rhus*), *129*, 135

Summer greens, 243

Summersweet (*Clethra alnifolia*), *63*

Sunken garden, 131

Sun-rose (*Helianthemum*), 37, 162

Sweet-alyssum (*Lobularia*), 89

Sweet marjoram (*Majorana hortensis*), 239, 243

Sweet-olive (*Osmanthus fragrans*), 4, 7, *12*, *63*, 227

Sweet-pea (*Lathyrus*), 13

Swiss chard, 243, 249

Swiss cheese vine (*Monstera*), *113*

Tamarisk (*Tamarix*), *129*, 131

Tamarix, 143

Taro root, tropical (*Colocasia esculenta*), *199*

Terrace, 111, 187

Texas ranger (*Leucophyllum*), 152

Thrift (*Armeria*), 89

Thrift, sea (*Armeria*), 5, 88, *127*, 135, 217, *218*

Thyme (*Thymus*), *127*, 239, 244
  golden, *144*
  woolly, 88, 99, 135, *144*, 152, 162

Ti, Hawaiian (*Cordyline*), *105*, 187, *193*

Tillandsia, *113*

Tomato (*Lycopersicon*), 240, 244
  'Atom' cherry, *241*
  cherry, 244

Torenia, 58

Tree, indoor, *175*, *178*, *181*, *183*, *184*, 187, *189*, *193*

Tree-of-heaven (*Ailanthus altissima*), 215

Trevesia palmata, *183*

Trillium, *51*, 58

Trinidad flame (*Calliandra*), *43*

Tropical planting, *195*, 195–215

Trumpetcreeper (*Campsis*), 28, 30

Trumpet vine, Chinese (*Campsis*), 28
  yellow, 28

Tulip (*Tulipa*), 3, *101*

Tupelo (*Nyssa*), *123*

Tupidanthus calyptratus, *183*

Turf-lily (*Liriope*), 227

Twinflower (*Linnaea*), *51*

Umbrella-palm (*Cyperus alternifolius*), 70, 165

Umbrella tree, Australian (*Brassaia*), *181*
  Queensland (*Brassaia*), 178

Vallisneria, 70

Vegetable, 243–244
  decorative, 244–249

Verbena, 131

Veronica (*Hebe*), *129*, 135

Viburnum, 7, *12*, *129*, 135
  blackhaw, *43*

Vine, 6, 13, 25, *26*, 27, 28, 29, 30, 39, 67, 99

Violet (*Viola*), 13, *51*, 58
  African, *140*

Virginia creeper (*Parthenocissus quinquefolia*), 6, 13, 30, 39, 42

Vriesia hieroglyphica, *113*

Walk, entry, 13–19, *101*

Wall, 25–50, *132*
  dry, 33, 160
  retaining, 30–33, 57, 159
  structure, 30

Wandering Jew (*Tradescantia*), 71, 187

Waterfall, 67, 72, 74, 75, 77, *108*, *157*, 227, 228

Water-hyacinth (*Eichhornia*), 70

Water-lettuce (*Pistia stratiotes*), 70

Water-lily (*Nymphaea*), 66, 68, 69, 81
  night-blooming tropical, 81
  pygmy, 70

Water-poppy (*Hydrocleys nymphoides*), 70

Wedelia trilobata, 135

Wild garden, 51

Willow (*Salix*), *51*, *123*
  alpine dwarf pussy, *141*
  goat, 135
  weeping, 222, 227

Wintercreeper (*Euonymus*), 28, 30
Wintergreen (*Gaultheria procumbens*), 58
Wisteria, 6, 13, 30, 32, 39, 42, 227
Witch-hazel (*Hamamelis*), 7
Woodruff, sweet (*Asperula odorata*), 58, 244
Wormwood (*Artemisia*), 162
  beach, 131

Yarrow, woolly (*Achillea*), 135, 162
Yesterday-today-and-tomorrow (*Brunfelsia calycina*), 12
Yew, English (*Taxus*), 33
Yucca tree, *11*, 70, 143, *151*, *152*, *256*

Zinnia, 131
Zoysia grass, 58
Zucchini, 243